MY SHIT LIFE SO FAR

FRANKIE BOYLE

HarperCollins*Publishers*

HarperCollins*Publishers*
77–85 Fulham Palace Road,
Hammersmith, London W6 8JB

www.harpercollins.co.uk

First published by HarperCollins*Publishers* 2009

3

© Frankie Boyle 2009

Frankie Boyle asserts the moral right to
be identified as the author of this work

A catalogue record of this book is
available from the British Library

HB ISBN 978-0-00-732449-1
TPB ISBN 978-0-00-732450-7

Printed and bound in Great Britain by
Clays Ltd, St Ives plc

All photographs have been supplied by the author, with the exception
of the following: BBC pp. 7 and 8 (bottom), Mirrorpix p. 11 (bottom),
Angst Productions Ltd pp. 14–16.

Mixed Sources
Product group from well-managed
forests and other controlled sources
www.fsc.org Cert no. SW-COC-1806
© 1996 Forest Stewardship Council
FSC

FSC is a non-profit international organisation established to promote the
responsible management of the world's forests. Products carrying the FSC
label are independently certified to assure consumers that they come
from forests that are managed to meet the social, economic and
ecological needs of present and future generations.

Find out more about HarperCollins and the environment at
www.harpercollins.co.uk/green

To all my enemies,
I will destroy you.

ACKNOWLEDGEMENTS

I would like to thank everybody at Chambers Management for standing between me and Chaos. I'm also very grateful to Treehouse and Mike and their mums for their patience and support. Also, it was very kind of Jim and Miles to let me include things I've written with them. I envy and pity them both for being so incredibly talented.

INTRODUCTION

I don't think anyone can have written an autobiography without at some point thinking, 'Why would anyone want to know this shit?' I've always read them thinking, 'I don't want to know where Steve Tyler grew up! Just tell me how many groupies he fucked!' I suppose I've just had to assume that anybody who buys this book has an interest in my life story, but I've covered myself by including long passages about all the groupies Steve Tyler has fucked.

I've been careful not to get too nostalgic. It's the most retrograde, reality-denying emotion. How long before you'll be standing at a bus stop hearing someone moan, 'Say what you like about Saddam, but that country's gone to hell without him'? Saddam did at least make the trains run on time. It's just that they were DeathTrains to DeathCamps. To be honest, they were often late but people were too scared to say anything.

There's a fair bit of swearing in this book. I wasn't going to put in any at all but then I thought, 'Fuck it, these readers are cunts.' I know there's an argument that swearing should only be used by a writer to underline a point that really demands it, or when strong emotions are in play. I think of this as a particularly English view, resting on the sad viewpoint that not much ever merits strong emotion or opinion. The whole debate is a bit pointless. I was in a hotel room recently and a show came on where Frank Skinner was talking about swearing on TV. I switched over and had a half-hearted wank. I'm one of about three people in the country directly affected, and I switched over. I would have happily watched Frank Skinner talk about anything else and I had a half-hearted wank over a presenter I know is a lesbian. For which I awarded myself double points.

There's a genuine BBC directive that says you can't use 'fucking' as a verb but you can use it as an adjective. So now you have to say, 'Do you know what's fucking great? Nookie!' Ian Wright has criticised the BBC for dumbing down. I agree with him, but there'd be more weight to his argument if he'd stayed with the BBC. I'm glad he escaped from the relentless intellectual slide to present *Gladiators*.

This book isn't entirely accurate. I have changed all the names and occasionally tweaked the order of events. I've also lied quite a lot. My favourite autobiography is Clive James's brilliant *Unreliable Memoirs*. In the introduction he says that all the stuff that sounds true is made up and all the unbelievable bits are true. I'm saying that too, stealing it from him. I also stole his Chapter Four, for anyone who wonders why I went to sixth-form college in Australia. There are a few other instances of plagiarism; they're mostly just the bits where I'm solving mysteries in Victorian London. Also, there are a couple of blatant untruths. The 1988 Scottish Cup Final was won by Celtic, rather than Dundee United, and I did not rape Tina Turner.

Sadly, there are parts of my life that haven't made it into the book. In the Seventies I was involved in a top-secret project. I'm not really allowed to talk about it, but it was big. That's all I can tell you about Operation C. I. AIDS. I went to some CIA seminars to begin with but I can't remember much about them. All I know is that anytime I hear any of John Lennon's solo stuff I go out and buy a harpoon. I still have the flask of Michael Jackson's DNA I stole for Operation Timberlake. His DNA wasn't hard to get. I dressed up as a schoolboy and hid the flask in my ass. I was also part of the plot to kill Castro, but it was impossible to get near him. I did manage to become his masseur, but even that he makes you do through a catflap with a snooker rest.

Being a special operative was a great job. How many people can say they got to meet all three Paul McCartneys? A lot of people wanted to strangle him after the Frog Chorus, but I was the one who actually got to do it. The CIA recruited me in an operation where they got prostitutes to spike people with acid and find out their secrets. They really had me over a barrel once they knew how much I liked to fuck prostitutes on acid.

There are quite a few drug-abuse stories coming up but I do urge you all to use drugs with caution. For example, never take cocaine before a group-therapy session. It's really hard to interrupt a discussion on incest with a great idea for a song. Also, never take opium suppositories. I've never been in a situation where I thought 'You know what would make this better? Hallucinating out of my arsehole.'

Another part of my life I've not been able to talk about is when I was spiritual adviser to the England football team. I had to leave because I just couldn't handle their attitude to women. You've got to worry when the movie on the team bus is *The Accused*. But you had to admire the simplicity of Sven's team talks. He'd simply stand in the dressing room and say, 'There are women out there.' The team wouldn't even leave by the door. They'd eat their way out onto the pitch through the dressing-room walls. Then for a while I ran an art project getting sex criminals and serial killers to send their ideas to television companies. It was always something they'd already thought of.

It's interesting for me to see the things people choose to get offended about and the things they let slide. Earlier this year I had to quit my *Daily Record* column over a moral disagreement. We disagreed over whether it was OK to make jokes about a dead child molester. It's not that I wasn't a fan of Michael Jackson – I was a big fan when I was 8. I didn't know it at the time, but I was his 'type'. For his London concerts Michael Jackson advertised for children in wheelchairs or with missing legs. What parent would agree to that? Look what happened to kids who could run away! Those tickets sold out in minutes. An interesting attitude we have to paedophilia in this country: 'We don't want paedophiles round here ... unless they've really worked on their choreography.'

We can all learn something from Michael's life. For example, it looks like oxygen tents are a big waste of money. Apparently when the news of his death broke, Jackson's father rushed straight to the hospital just to check if the medics needed a hand with beating Michael's chest. The man may be gone but he has left a musical legacy that will be around for hundreds of years. As will his face.

There's a really grim pro-censorship lobby that seems to be thriving at the moment. The *Daily Mail* and these religious maniacs must be stopped. They won't rest until all telly has been cleansed. Until there's no swearing and *Walking with Dinosaurs* is exposed as the heretical lie it is. They'll be Walking with Creationists – 'Our story begins 7,000 years ago when God created the earth – exactly like it is today. Here's a Tyrannosaurus rex, being buried by God to test our faith.' These are the same nutcases who complained that having Fiona Bruce present *Antiques Roadshow* was disgraceful and encouraged lustful thoughts. Presumably while all wanking like an incarcerated rapist on ecstasy.

It's been interesting to write a book and work without the hands-on censorship of TV and radio. Amusingly, amidst all the horror of the world, I was censured this year for daring to make a joke about Israel. I think it was, 'I've been studying Israeli Army Martial Arts. I now know sixteen ways to kick a Palestinian woman in the back.' I was pulled up about this as civilians were killed by Israeli troops in Gaza. This was on a show called *Political Animal* on Radio 4. That's where producers like to focus the edginess in their shows into the title.

But what I find incredible is that the Israelis say they can build housing in the West Bank because the Palestinians weren't productive enough with it. So if a bunch of settlers start building flats on your back patio you've only got yourself to blame. For fuck's sake plant some marrows before it's too late. People say nothing can solve the Middle East problem. Not mediation, not arms, not financial aid. I say there is Something. Atheism. Suddenly everyone would be looking at each other thinking, 'What the fuck were we doing? That was insane! Why are we all wearing these ridiculous hats? Were we drunk?' Also, you could eliminate the problem of suicide bombing overnight by making everybody wear spandex. Good old Israel. They're the South Africa that it's not OK to call cunts. Mind you, I don't understand the Palestinians either. If they hate Israel so much why don't they go form their own fucking country?

It's not like I don't get offended myself. I was horrified last year when some people said the floods were God's judgements on homosexuals. That's an outrageously offensive thing to say, especially when everyone knows that God's actual judgement was AIDS. But it's often the most innocuous jokes that make TV bosses go nuts; there really isn't any logic to it. Once I made a joke about Prince Harry, saying that now he'd joined the army he could look forward to having an arsehole like a collapsed mineshaft. A woman from the channel literally ran onto the studio floor screaming 'Nooooo!' in a strange, slow-motion way and waving her hands in the air like somebody about to get eaten by a giant bug on *Dr Who*. But don't feel sorry for Harry. The initiations and rituals in the army must be a light relief compared with those in the royal family. In the army it's just drinking and getting hit on the backside with a cricket bat. No altar. No lizards from the lower fourth dimension. No having to watch your grandmother dislocate her jaw to consume a terrified homeless teenager. Harry actually has a lot in common with the average squaddy. In that he has absolutely no idea who his real father is.

That said, I don't really understand the point of the royal princes joining the army. Why send a couple of pampered party boys like Harry or William in to fight? In a war you need a ruthless, merciless killing machine, someone like Andy McNab, or Prince Philip. Prince Philip is the perfect soldier: he likes shooting things and he's a racist. He'd kill his own daughter-in-law if he thought he could get away with it.

It's amazing how difficult it is to get jokes onto TV shows when adverts for abortions are to be shown on television. I wonder if they will use more famous adverts as inspiration. Have a break, have a killed kid. Or the McDonald's classic, 'I'm not lovin' it.' I suppose the best advert for abortion is just a silent thirty-second shot of Chris Moyles. The first TV advert for the morning-after pill has already been shown. It's just a clip of the *Teletubbies* and a voice saying, 'If you don't want to watch this shit – take the pill!'

Having looked back over my career while writing this, I've concluded that show business is a great thing to work in, particularly if you enjoyed the stories of H. P. Lovecraft. Paul Gascoigne is appearing in a TV show called *Total Wipeout*. This is cruel. I don't know if you've seen Gazza recently but he looks like he emits a high-pitched shriek at 1 am every morning that kills all the insects within ten miles. Judging by the title I assume it's just Gazza staring at the screen attached to a saline drip, silently whispering the words to 'Fog on the Tyne' as someone performs brain surgery on him with an ice-cream scoop. Actually, it sounds like a winner.

Pretty much every celebrity nowadays seems to be a satirical morality tale. When Peter Andre left Jordan she was said to be devastated. Now she's left with only two massive tits. Peter escaped to Cyprus; it says something when you escape the arguments and fighting by going to an island with UN peacekeepers. But he will of course be entitled to half of Jordan's assets, so at least he gets a spacehopper out of it. And Kerry Katona announced on Facebook that she is selling off one of her breast implants on eBay in a bid to raise money for charity. One of them? What is she doing with the other one? Letting it look after the kids? I'm surprised Kerry is on Facebook, although I suppose it's one way she can keep in touch with her children.

It's easy to lose your sense of perspective in show business. I totally understand why people end up doing things they really shouldn't. Apart from anything else, people keep offering them money. Nadya Suleman, the mother who gave birth to octuplets earlier this year, was offered £700,000 to appear in a porn film.

Fair enough – she's had more people inside her than most porn stars. Whoever the male star is, I hope he has GPS or he might not find his way out again. You can't really describe it as throwing a sausage up an alley; it'll be more like flicking a grain of rice into outer space. After having eight babies, is a penis really going to do it for her? I think she'll need a football team in scuba gear armed with ostrich feathers and power tools.

I know show business seems fucking pointless now, like something Hieronymus Bosch coughed into a hankie. Look in your heart, though, you know that it's going to get worse. We'll look back on Tom Cruise as a charming eccentric. The actor who replaces him as the No.1 film promotion entity will probably worship a giant serpent, marry Hermione from Harry Potter and lay an egg in her chest.

It's been fun becoming a micro-celebrity just as the whole idea of fame gets debased by reality-show contestants. Once, getting recognised in the street put you on a par with Grace Kelly. Now it puts you in the same bracket as somebody who attempted to beat the world ferret-stamping record on *Britain's Got Talent*. Susan Boyle is now so famous that a Croatian TV crew were filming her in Scotland. They wondered which ethnic war could have caused so much desolation. Then a café owner said he saw her face in a slice of toast. So what? Every day I see her face in my toilet bowl. Everyone keeps asking me if Susan Boyle is a relative. Of course not – none of them will ever manage to chisel their way out of that cellar. I suppose we do have things in common; I look ridiculous dressed as a woman too. Come on, Susan Boyle does look uncannily like Mrs Doubtfire as played by Gordon Brown. She had a lot of people laughing at her because of her looks, but what people don't realise is that she's probably one of the best-looking people in West Lothian.

I can't make too many jokes about Susan Boyle as the British public have taken her to their heart. What can I say? Britain loves a dog. Sorry, underdog. Let's be honest and say that God broke the mould, just before he made her. Susan claims she has never been kissed. On that evidence alone, Scotland's alcohol problems are not nearly as bad as previously imagined. OK, so she hasn't been kissed, but this is Scotland. I'll bet she's been fingered on a school trip to Largs. There are probably thousands of Susan Boyles out there who were worried about coming forward in case they got laughed at – and let's just hope her success doesn't change that. Still, congratulations to the third most talented Boyle in Scotland. I'm number two and first place goes to my uncle Jim, who can play the flute from four different orifices.

You can gauge the success of any Scottish celebrity by how much they are hated in Scotland. By these standards I am still pretty much plankton. A side effect of micro-celebrity is that you do get hit on by a lot of hoaxers. I had a wee boy phone me up the other day and pretend to be my long-lost son. All I can say to that little lad is that he'll have to get up a lot earlier in the morning if he wants to get his hands on my bone marrow.

In any case, the whole of television and celebrity is simply a distraction aimed at keeping you sedated while your pockets are picked by vested interests that may or may not be lizards. You're going to end up with celebrity reality shows piped directly into your eyes the same way that classical music is played to fatten cattle. What kind of person buys the autobiography of a panel-show contestant? Wake up you CUNT.

ONE

I grew up in Glasgow. It's a disturbing but strangely loveable place, lurching like any alcoholic from exuberance to unbelievable negativity. I always loved the hilariously downbeat motto, 'Here's the Bird that Never Flew. Here's the Tree that Never Grew. Here's the Bell that Never Rang. Here's the Fish that Never Swam.' It's like the city slogan that got knocked back by Hiroshima. They might as well have a coat of arms where St Mungo hangs himself from a disused crane.

We lived in a place called Pollokshaws. It was an aching cement void, a slap in the face to Childhood, and for the family it was a step up.

Until I was about three we had lived in the Gorbals, a pretty run-down bit that got knocked down as soon as we left. I've still got a few memories of it. Standing out in the back, while a wee boy with a grubby face lit matches. He let them burn down to his fingertips while I stood there thinking, 'This is one of those bad boys Mum keeps telling me about.' I remember Mum giving me money in a sweetshop to pay the man behind the counter and just throwing the coins at his surprised face. And I have a vivid memory of being with my brother and finding an old tin sign that advertised ice-creams and lollies, the kind that creaks in the wind. We loved it so much that we kept it outside our front door. When we got back from holiday with Mum that summer, my dad said it had been stolen and we were in tears. We'd been talking all the way home about how much we were looking forward to getting back and seeing our sign. In retrospect, Dad obviously fucked it onto a rubbish tip.

My dad was a labourer. There had been a building strike starting the day I was born and he'd been planning on joining it. I imagine my mum probably had something to say about him walking out of his job as she gave birth. He did the honourable thing: feigning sciatica and getting a three-week sick line. After my sister came along he was able to put our name down for a new council house, move us to somewhere a bit more child-friendly. He went for a place a little further down the Gorbals because it was near his work. This is the last recorded instance of him using his own judgement. Mum went screaming across town like an artillery shell, landing in the housing department and refusing to leave until they gave us a flat in the Shaws.

One of the first things I did after we moved in was, aged 3, to eat a whole bottle of painkillers that my mum had hidden in a cupboard. I had thought they were her secret supply of sweeties. I was rushed to hospital and had my stomach pumped. There they discovered that I had also scoffed a packet of rusks and these had prevented the painkillers from hitting my stomach and killing me. Saved by my own greed!

*   *   *

I already showed a general talent for the offensive non sequitur at this age. My parents introduced me to a friend of theirs who was over from Ireland. I'd never met her before but listened to her pronouncements on what a big boy I was, before sailing in with,

'I saw you washing your bum in the bath last night.'

She was quite a shy, demure lady so there was a sort of choked silence and then we went our different ways.

Our house was part of a tenement: six flats linked by a communal stairway (called a close) with four big back gardens divided by fences but linked by the traffic of stray cats and children. This is where adults dried their washing and dumped their rubbish in a concrete midden. Where we built dens and dug holes and captured wee beasties and killed them.

One major feature of my childhood was how cold the house was. The only heating was a three-bar gas fire in the living room that went on for the 6 O'Clock News. My mum would sit on the floor with her legs running across it lengthways and the kids would all sit at right angles with their legs over hers. I had a constant cold, despite there being enough blankets on my bed that I could have comfortably survived a gunshot. Sometimes the fire would go on in the morning before nursery and I'd heat my clothes up in front of it and roast my legs until there were red swirling patterns all the way up to my shorts.

When I was growing up I think most people struggled with what we'd now call 'fuel poverty'. The price of fuel rose twice as fast in Scotland as in the rest of Europe. Hello! Those big pointy things in the water are called fucking oil rigs. Scotland is basically a huge lump of coal with roads and Tesco Metros on top. I hate to say it but we're a nation of suckers. We tell our old people to wear an extra jumper in winter. They should be watching the Queen's Speech in a thong, warming their mince pies by the glow of a sixteen-bar fire.

My childhood came near the end of that clichéd time when you knew everybody in your close. An old couple called the Robinsons across from us on the ground floor had a grandson who could draw. When he visited them I would love to sit and watch him conjure cars and dogs and boxers with a piece of charcoal. Upstairs from us were the Patons, a family cruelly held back by a society that didn't sufficiently reward bad tempers, heavy footedness and shouting. Across from them was Mrs Heinz, a kind old lady with a face like a tiny withered apple. The top landing had a pompous fool of a newsagent who had his initials stencilled across the driver door of his Toyota Corolla and opposite him a wee man called Norrie who was, in no particular order, a communist, golfer and homosexual.

Pollokshaws in general was a lot like *Bladerunner* without the special effects. Turning one way from our house, high rises towered over freezing little Sixties prefabs. The other way, the road must have been one of the bleakest in Europe: on it were a yard filled with building materials that was eternally locked up, a tiny office building the size of a large van and a milk factory. All facing a giant used-car lot. I spent a lot of my childhood terrified of nuclear war. Every time I heard a plane go overhead I was convinced we were all about to disappear in a ball of incendiary light. Handily, the car lot had a terrifying alarm system that went off every other night and sounded quite a lot like a 6-year-old's idea of the four-minute warning.

In the centre of Pollokshaws was an underground shopping centre where shops struggled to stay open. Not the bookies or the boozer that were in there; they did fine. Food was just less of an essential. The W of 'Pollokshaws Shopping Centre' had been stolen long ago and replaced with a shaky, spray-painted 'G' under which old ladies would stand around nattering, taking a sweepstake on which of their friends would last the winter. In the dead centre of it all was a memorial to the Scottish socialist John McLean, who would have wept.

You had to be careful going through here with your mum. If she saw someone she knew, you'd have to stand disconsolately by her side while they exchanged information about prices and graphic descriptions of the illnesses of mutual acquaintances. It might as well have been in another language. My mum spoke Irish, so it often was.

There were maybe half a dozen high flats in the area. Most tower blocks in the Seventies were so depressing they should have put a diving board on the roof. I think Scottish architects in the Sixties must have been given massive bribes by the makers of lithium. The way they'd been positioned meant that the main street, Shawbridge Street, was essentially a wind tunnel. My brother used to walk me to school when I was very little (he'd make me walk about five steps behind, so people didn't know I was with him). One day we got caught up in a wind so fierce that I lifted right up into the air. I hovered briefly, about four feet up, like a tiny superhero who had foolishly attempted to strike fear into criminals with a duffel-coat costume. The wind stopped suddenly and I landed right on my face. I was really proud of my torn trousers and gashed leg – a proper injury!

There was a bit behind one of the high flats that got so windy that nobody could hear you if you shouted into the wind. Well, you couldn't hear yourself; I don't know if anybody else could hear. Maybe everybody round there dreaded blustery days because random children would turn up and scream obscenities outside their windows. To be honest, we did that on sunny days too.

I got a telescope when I was a bit older. Actually my brother got a telescope that he never used. I'd train it on the windows of the upper storeys and look at folk – there were a couple of buildings that you could see right into. I think I was partly hoping to see women's tits, inspired by a scene in *Gregory's Girl*, but it was largely just curiosity. There was a couple who'd always dance together, drunk. It was sweet and a little bit sordid.

One of my favourites was this woman (although I thought of her as an old woman, she was probably mid-30s) who'd do really high-powered Eighties aerobics and then put on a coat and go outside onto the balcony and smoke fags for ages, just looking down into the street. Once a guy had jumped out of that high flat and hit one of the concrete posts at the bottom where we used to play leapfrog. It never really got cleaned up properly and he became an impressively large stain that lasted for years. As a kid, I wondered if this woman was thinking about jumping. I wondered why this guy had jumped and distrusted my dad's explanation ('He was drunk'). As a teenager I grew really disgusted with the area. I'd look up at the flimsy little net curtains in the windows as I walked home from the library every night, wondering why we didn't all jump.

My favourite window was right at the top of a block on Shawbridge Street. A guy did martial arts in his living room wearing a sort of ninja outfit. It's hard to be precise, but it looked like an all-black bodysuit and maybe a balaclava. He had nunchakus and a wooden sword and he'd be there every night – occasionally you could even see him leaping about with the lights off. I was visiting my parents years later when I was at uni and thought that I must just have dreamt this guy. I got out the same old telescope and pointed it up at his window. Ten years later and he was still there. Looked like he'd gotten really good at it too.

The high rise nearest us had a bunch of shops set into the basement. The main one was an Asian newsagent that constantly changed hands as shopkeepers weighed up the cost of cleaning graffiti against the profit margin on a chocolate tool. When I was little there was a Sixties-style soda bar which had somehow survived into a completely different era. It was run by two old ladies with big beehive hairdos and they sold ice-cream floats and milkshakes, very, very slowly. It closed when one of them died. I remember one of the local mums telling me about it when we were coming home from school one day. I asked what had happened to her and the woman grunted, 'Her liver went.'

We always got our hair cut at this barber called 'Old Hughie's'. Old Hughie was from the Islands somewhere, was always completely pished and had a wooden leg. My mum would sit balefully behind us as we sat in the chair, encouraging him to take more hair off. She always left bitterly disappointed that we still had a little hair. Pretty much the only cut that would have satisfied her would have exposed a sizeable section of our brains.

The place had a history of housing immigrants from way back. There was an old song about the time it had consisted of a whole load of Flemish people in the nineteenth century called 'The Queer Folk o' the Shaws'. The place had stayed pretty queer. There was a library and a swimming pool and that was it. On the hill at the far end of town was our church, the church hall and school. All built on a hill screened by trees. John Stirling Maxwell, who owned the area, had allowed Catholics to build those only if they were somewhere he couldn't see them.

At the time religious division in Glasgow seemed absolute. It was brutal too. When I was just a little kid a Celtic player electrocuted himself by accident in his loft. 'It's My Party and I'll Cry if I Want To' was number one and on the radio, and at that week's football you could hear the Rangers fans singing 'It's My Attic and I'll Fry if I Want To'. A Rangers player called Tom McKean gassed himself in his car and the graffiti was 'Gas 1, McKean 0'.

I remember getting my tonsils out when I was a wee lad and I made friends with a Protestant boy on my ward. Neither of us could sleep the night before our operations and we sat up watching trains going by out of the window. The city underneath us seemed dark and wonderful. We were up till morning, watching tiny silhouettes go to their work. When my dad asked me what I'd done in hospital I said, 'I spoke to a Protestant.' It just seemed much stranger than anything else that had happened.

I was also born with what used to be called 'bat ears' – protruding ears with no folds in them. At secondary school these would have been the equivalent of having 'Insert Cock Here' tattooed on my chin but the primary-school kids weren't too bad about it. I think there was a huge waiting list to get an operation but somehow my mum managed to persuade a surgeon to do it quickly. He was genuinely doing it off the books or something, like a mechanic might have a look at his mate's motor after hours. Afterwards, I had to wear pads over my ear for weeks, secured with a big hairnet. Well, that's what it looked like to me. To everyone at school it seemed to say, 'Please slap or punch me in the ears.' I was supposed to go back a couple of years later and get my lobes pinned back as well. Unfortunately, the guy had selfishly died in the interval so I've still got these weird protruding lobes. Who knows how many jobs this bloke was knocking off in his lunch hour, out of the goodness of his heart? I often look at people with big earlobes in Scotland and wonder if we're all part of some perverse brotherhood.

The bit of Pollokshaws we lived in wasn't a bad place for wee boys and girls. The sort of things that horrify estate agents are pretty good for kids. There was a big bit of waste ground nearby and people didn't seem to mind you digging big holes in the grass or building dens in the trees. A den meant dragging sheets of wood, plastic or whatever you could find up against the body of the tree and then boldly proclaiming it a den, rather than building anything. Once we found a load of discarded doors and used them to completely surround a tree, creating a plywood armadillo. You had to jump into it, nobody having thought to use one of the doors as a door.

I had an older brother, John, and a younger sister, Karen. I shared a room with John, and Karen had a room of her own. John was a slightly nervous little boy, always worrying about what our parents would say or what they'd think he should do in any situation. We used to say our prayers every night before bed and then we'd talk a bit as we fell asleep. I always remember him turning to me one night and saying:

'There's always one thing that you're worrying about. You stop worrying about one thing and you worry about something else. It never stops.'

I lay awake. It was the first thing I'd heard that had genuinely worried me.

For years my brother's school day started before mine and in theory I should have been able to sleep for an extra hour. He hated getting up though and my mum would have to stand over him, shouting his name in a weird trembling soprano while I

buried my head under the covers. He was like a comic-book cari-
cature of a sleepy boy. Crust would form on his eyes and he'd
struggle to open them while he pulled apart his breakfast of jam
sandwiches. Then he'd climb back into bed with all his clothes in
his arms and twitch endlessly under the covers like Harry Houdini
before emerging fully clothed.

My brother and sister and I all made friends with the twins in
the next back, Thomas and Rosemary Duffy, and there were other
kids you'd see as their families moved through the area, or as
they came to visit relatives. Wee people had a much more
autonomous life then, going out on their own and knowing they
had to be back for lunch and dinner.

At any time there'd be seven or eight of us knocking around
out in the backs. Rosemary was a sweet lassie who loved to feed
and name all the rogue cats. Thomas had a gruesome streak, so
we got on tremendously. We'd drop snails from the top of the
tenements, seeing whose could survive the longest, like an evil
game of conkers. We dug a massive hole in my back and when
nobody came to stop us we just kept going. It was right up the
far end so the adults couldn't really see us from their windows.
After about three or four days somebody must have noticed we
were exhausted, coming home filthy and coughing like miners. I
remember a shocked figure looming over us, buried up to our
chests and probably heading for the water mains.

Wee Thomas had an inspired idea for the hole. A lesser boy
would have pulled a sheet of tarpaulin over it and called it a den.
But Thomas staged what he called 'Insect Disaster Movies'. This

meant that you got down into the hole with a set of binoculars while Thomas laid worms or ants or snails before you. You were to look at them through the binoculars (backwards) while he rolled stones onto them, doing the voices of the fleeing beasties as they screamed their horror and worried aloud which way to run to flee the earthquake.

The Duffys had an enormous Alsatian. Once I went round for them and Rosemary opened the door only to suddenly disappear, this monstrous thing dragging her up the hall by her ankle. Their dad, 'Old Tom', was my dad's drinking partner, although who knows what they talked about. My dad was quiet but Old Tom was almost silent. The few things he did say were delivered in such a low, worried Glasgow burr that it sounded like somebody asking for help through faulty air conditioning. My dad told me that they went to a country and western bar once, one of these unbelievable places in Glasgow where people dress as cowboys. Some guy came up and started showing them his quick-draw skills and gun twirling. 'I've been timed as having a faster draw than John Wayne!', he told them, just as he dropped the gun. In one of his few recorded utterances, Old Tom looked at him and deadpanned.

'If John Wayne was here now, you'd be deid.'

One day all of the kids were sitting on the stairs in the Duffys close and the idea got thrown up that we should form a gang. The girls wanted us to call it 'The Mickey Mouse Club'. The boys had come up with 'The Bloodsucking Slugs'. Actually, that was my idea. We made my sister cry at the horror of being a

Bloodsucking Slug. That day finished with Rosemary Duffy tying me to a washing pole and saying she was going to kiss me. I struggled with the washing line tied round me but I really wanted her to kiss me. Somehow I got free anyway and ran off, hopping disappointedly over the railings into my own back.

Thomas Duffy and I both joined the Cubs, which we loved. I think we'd exaggerated the subs to our folks so we could buy Slush Puppies on the way home. Our parents never caught on, even though we'd always come back with bright blue or purple mouths and crippling headaches. The Cubs was run by a lovely lady who lived round the corner from us. I don't think she knew a single thing about the Cubs or the Scouting movement; she just started it up in the church hall to give us something to do. There were none of the awkward formal greetings and knot tying of the proper Cubs. If you wanted a badge you just told her and she'd set you a totally arbitrary task. I got my sports badge for running round the hall. There was a great fancy-dress competition every Halloween. Once I went as the Hulk – painted from head to foot in watercolours that dried on me in such a way that I seemed to be walking around in a huge scab. Thomas, quite brilliantly, painted an enormous cardboard box and went as an Oxo cube. He made his dad walk us to the hall as he had a real paranoia that a passing lunatic might set fire to him.

The Cub leader's brother would come to the meetings a lot to help out; he was maybe in his twenties. The last 20 minutes of most meetings involved him tying an enormous running shoe to a big bit of rope and making us jump as he swung it round faster and faster. Who knows what was going on in this guy's life that he'd turn up every week to blast wee boys into the side of a public building with an enormous shoe, but we were really glad that he did. I even won one week! I was encouraged to stage a high-jump competition at some railings near our house, hurting my balls quite badly.

Our outfit or unit or whatever (not having been in the proper Cubs, who knows what the term is) went to a real Scout camp once and it was absolute chaos. There's always been something suspect about Scoutmasters to me. Middle-aged men taking young boys into the woods to practise tying knots is clearly not good. If you're going to get felt up in a tent by the Scoutmaster then the very least you should get is a badge that you can use to cover the hole in the back of your shorts.

There was also some weird sectarian thing going on with the guy who was leading the trip. I was too young to decode what was going on but when the kids started singing 'Flower of Scotland' on the bus he went absolutely tonto, making the driver pull into a lay-by and giving a truly crazy, bulging-eyed speech about the Queen. That's a real thing with sectarians – they always assume that people are interested in the shite they talk. He was literally foaming at the mouth about the Act of Union, in front of a bunch of 9-year-olds who were thinking about when they might get a hotdog. Of course one must avoid generalisations but that man was definitely a paedophile.

At camp, we were no more prepared to set up tents and light fires than a tribe of monkeys. In fact, one of our guys (a real wingnut who seemed much too tall and old to be a Cub) immediately climbed a tree and started screaming like a monkey, breaking off branches and throwing them into the camp. Another got off the bus and just ran straight down towards the river bank, crashing straight into the river. The real Scouts looked shell-shocked as the monkey guy leapt down from the tree and tried to engage them in swordfights with an enormous stick. Clearly, all pretence of being a real outfit, unit or possibly troop had been blown.

The Scouts sent an observer to one of our meetings. I missed it but apparently he stood around slack-jawed watching boys get pelted into stacks of chairs with a big training shoe. We were all made to attend a real Cubs meet in a better part of town. The Cubs had to line up and do a little salute at the start! The leader was called Akela! The gymnastics badge didn't simply require jumping two-footed over a chair! Their leader called out a boy to give a mad little speech about the history of Scouting. He had an enormous gum boil, easily half the size of his face, and spoke in a wet mumble like the Elephant Man Jr. The meetings must have been bad because our Cubs got shut down and there was fuck all to do again.

In a way crime makes perfect sense in those nothing-to-do places. A teenager came up to us once on a moped he'd stolen and said he'd give us rides on the back of it. I was too scared but some of the kids got on for a backie. I still have this vivid picture of him shooting off across the waste ground at the end. He might have been the last truly free individual I ever met and is no doubt dead.

I had a rich fantasy life as a kid, honed on the dullness of my surroundings. I read *The Hobbit* when I was little and after that every magic-type kids' book that I could find. I loved Alan Garner and Diana Wynne-Jones, and just read that stuff all the time.

My own fantasies were a whole lot weirder than anything in the books. I had this baroque story that I thought about for years. I'd go off and play on my own, thinking about it and acting out the scenes. I was a magician who travelled from town to town in some Middle Earth-type world with his travelling companion who – get this – was an enormous guy that he had created from mud. My companion, whose name escapes me, was always falling to pieces and I'd have to redo the spells. He had rubies for eyes – not any old rubies, but magic rubies that I stored powerful fire spells in. The stories largely involved the two of us rocking up to town and not getting any respect from the local king or whoever. He'd generally try to put us in jail or set his men on us. That's when my good buddy would unleash all the pent-up rage in his fiery eye, often burning not just the king and his men but the whole town that had disrespected us.

But here's the best bit. I had a sword that would cut whoever it touched and give them a wound that would never heal. I think I must have read about that somewhere. In some versions of the story, I had cut myself with the sword, all down one arm, so my arm was hidden and bandaged in my cloak and I was often weak. The story regularly revolved around me trying to rest up while we were in prison or being chased. My fiery friend would stand guard over me while I summoned up enough energy to destroy our enemies. Later on in life, this made my national stand-up tour feel pretty familiar.

My brother and sister and I were allowed to get one comic each a week. We'd get *The Victor* and *The Dandy* and sometimes others. I was never one for savouring the artwork; I just loved the stories. My favourite in *The Victor* was a thing called 'Deathwish'. It was about a racing driver and sometime stunt-man who had been horribly disfigured in a crash. He wore a mask to cover his injuries and basically longed for death. Each week he'd try to do something in the race or stunt he was work-ing on to kill himself. It always backfired and helped him win his race or do an amazing stunt, much to his disappointment. There was a brilliant panel once of him coming to in his hospital bed to the sound of popping champagne corks, just lying there look-ing disgusted.

I'd plough through our comics quickly and read my sister's *Bunty* when nobody was looking. It had a lot of weird stuff. 'Susan the Sham' was great: a girl who'd been in a traffic acci-dent and had an evil uncle who was making her pretend to be deaf for compensation reasons. Every week she'd overhear some-thing she really ought to tell somebody about but couldn't. One of the main stories – did I dream this? – was about a lassie who lived a pretty much normal life except for one thing. She was trapped inside an enormous energy ball. She'd go to school in it and have to deal with a certain amount of hassle but when it got too much she could always just shoot off into the sky in this fiery orb. I once tried to make a sketch about this for a pilot I was doing. The producer read the script and then said one of my favourite-ever sentences:

'Do you know how much of our budget it would take to create an energy ball?'

That's the great thing about television. Sometimes, you just feel that anything could happen. The guy didn't say it was impossible. He was just thinking of the repercussions of sticking an actress in a big, glowing energy ball!

A new comic came out that was an absolute mindblower. *The Buddy* it was called. Cheery title but a clue to its disturbing nature was in the human-skull jacket pin given away with the first issue and the lead story of 'They Saved Hitler's Brain!' They had Limpalong Leslie, an international footballer with one leg shorter than the other. His footballing brain always had to be working overtime as he was essentially crippled. He'd leap over tackles saying, 'Ho ho! He telegraphed that one!' It was still less weird than Tuffy, the story of a homeless goalkeeper. He could never find a house, even during the couple of seasons he played for Spurs.

I felt outside of the stuff the other kids were into, like the whole football thing. I support Celtic but as I got older I struggled to see those clubs as anything other than big businesses making money out of some of the poorest people in society. You go to those grounds and they're these giant chrome fortresses rising out of blighted, deprived communities. Celtic won the European Cup in 1967 with a team all born within five miles of the ground. If they tried that now they couldn't find eleven guys who still had two legs. I find it difficult to believe that people can care about whether some millionaire pervert has got a thigh strain or not. That's another thing about football – it's a bit gay. Guys fretting over some lad's calf or hamstring – they might as well all fuck each other in the centre circle.

Both of the Old Firm clubs have profited massively from sectarianism. Personally, I think everyone involved over the years has shown that they don't have Northern Ireland's best interests at heart and it should now be given to a third party, like Spain. Imagine how little the average Belfast citizen would care for the problems of religion if he could just get a nice bit of tapas on the Falls Road. And it wasn't fucking raining all the time. And he still had knees.

The standard of football has been pretty terrible for a long time. There have been some great sides but they're pretty rare. Most of the time the Scottish League is like watching a really gruelling donkey race. Sure, like most people I support one team over another, but it's getting more and more difficult to care what colour of hat the winning donkey is wearing.

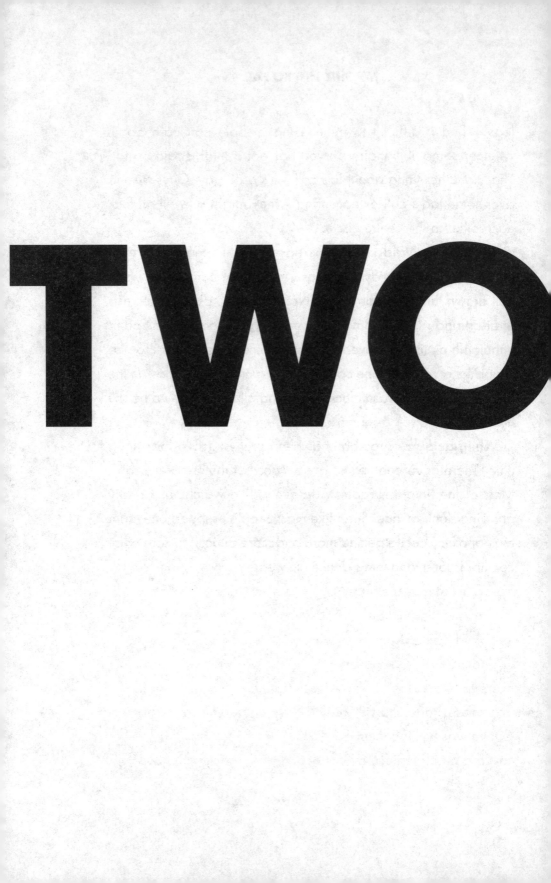

TWO

Primary school was great. On the first day I was looking around thinking, 'There's no catch ... this is genuinely a big, warm room full of toys.' Now, Little Frankie would have hated it if he knew that one day I was going to gloss over his nursery education, which he absolutely loved. On the other hand, books can only be so long and I've got a lot of stories about drug abuse to get to. Let's just say that Little Frankie pulled the paddling pool off its stand about once a month, soaking himself and having to go home in a pair of huge borrowed shorts.

The great thing about primary education is the positivity and praise the kids get. Probably not the best way to prepare them for the reality of adult life in Scotland, but I like it. I think if we actually focussed on an education system that prepared people for life in Scotland it would be a lot like the Fritzl household. I mean, what gets me about this whole sordid story is Fritzl's wife saying she didn't know. Did she not suspect something when her husband came in every week with sixteen bags of shopping, including kids' clothes and nappies? Who did she think they were for – the dog? 'I know we treat him like one of the family, but sandals and shorts?' People have accused Fritzl of neglect, but he was fucking them every day – they probably would have loved a bit of neglect. Even Adolf Hitler must be going, '... und

I thought *Ich war ein Cunt!*' The whole thing is so common in Austria they now sell 'Hallmark' cards with 'Congratulations on escaping from your underground sex hell'. Of course, I shouldn't joke; Fritzl's daughter has been through a horrific ordeal. But just wait until she gets all the back payments for child benefit. That'll cheer her up.

I loved primary and it was so supportive that up until I was about 9 or 10 I still thought I could draw. Teachers had always said, 'Well done' when I drew or painted something, so I didn't realise that I couldn't draw at all – almost to the level of a handicap. This dawned on me when I challenged my friend Charlie to a drawing contest. We were going to draw a space shuttle as it was the first one and the kids were really excited about it. I used a ruler and drew a big rectangle in the middle and two bigger rectangles on either side, for the booster jets. Then I drew triangles on top of the rectangles – turning them into rockets! Sure, the space shuttle that I drew freehand inside the main rectangle (the fuel tank!) was a little shaky and looked a bit like a face, but the overall effect was pretty impressive.

Charlie blinked impassively at my drawing and then produced what seemed to be a black and white photograph of the space shuttle. There were little scientists doing final checks on the scaffolding at the launch base, partially covered by the shadow of the main fuel tank. Did you ever read *Peanuts* when Charlie Brown would be building his shitty little snow fort and

Linus would have built an actual castle with battlements and a flagpole? It was like that. I insisted mine was best and went off to find a judge.

As a kid I was fascinated by space shuttles and by astronauts in general. This was before all the blowing up took the shine off things. Good old NASA. With all their money, could they maybe have a mission where everyone doesn't nearly die? They should have some honesty and call their next mission 'Operation Spacegrave'. Remember all the unmanned missions they used to send up in the 1950s and 60s? You know what they did with the monkeys and dogs that piloted them? They poisoned them! All their bodies are still up there. So an alien civilisation's first contact with earth will be a ring of abandoned spacecraft filled with dead chimps and Alsatians. Approaching earth for some sublimated alien race must be like when the police close in on the house of a serial killer and find an outer perimeter of faeces wrapped in newspaper.

One day on our way to school my friend Gary McRedie and I found a huge porn mag. It was thicker than a dictionary and full of big Seventies bushes – women who looked like they were giving birth to Kevin Keegan. I didn't really understand what it was (I don't think), but had to admit it was strangely compelling. Gary suggested that we hide it under a shrub so we could come and look at it whenever we liked. The next day it was gone – someone had found it! I was disappointed but also oddly relieved. It was only years later, as I was telling someone this story, that I realised Gary McCredie had gone back and got it for himself.

There was quite a lot of religious stuff at primary. Every week we'd go down to the church and practise hymns, led by Miss Moat, a spirited big woman who looked like she played centre-back for somebody half decent. At least I was lucky enough not to go to a Jesuit school. The Jesuit saying is 'Give me a boy until he is seven and I will give you the man.' Usually a sexually confused manic-depressive.

We made our first confession when we were seven years old and had to really rack our brains for sins. I said that I'd stolen something, which I hadn't, and that I'd lied, which I had – about stealing something. An old man listening to a child's sins while they're both locked in a wooden box? If I was a sexual pervert I would definitely join the priesthood. Although clearly the sexual-pervert community is way ahead of me on that one. Earlier this year the Pope met victims of sexual abuse at the hands of Catholic priests. If I'd been fingered by a priest the last person I'd like to meet is the ultra priest 9,000. It's like fighting the end-of-level boss in a video game. First confession at the age of seven must be incredibly boring for the priest. Imagine having to listen for hours on end about stealing conkers and farting during school assembly. This is why so many priests like to help out by giving the poor kid something to really confess about next time around.

First holy communion was the big one – all the girls dressing up in terrifying tiny bridal outfits to trot up the aisle and 'marry God'. It was a whole community doing this. If one guy had made a kid do that in his basement he'd have been locked up for life. I lost both my front teeth during the week of my first communion so my smile in the photos is the tight-lipped smirk of an unrepentant murder suspect. I always remember the present I was given for making my first communion. It was the biography of a terminally Christian boy with cerebral palsy. It was called *I Won't Be Crippled When I See Jesus*. I put *Emil and the Detectives* to one side and read it every night with a sense of numb horror.

I've always found it weird that people in our community could reconcile the opulence of the Church (even our little church was disgracefully beautiful compared with the houses people lived in) with the generally held socialism that most folk seemed to believe in. I remember a visiting priest giving an angry sermon about communism and lots of men getting up and quietly walking out. Often priests will give a homily about the evils of greed in a room with more gold and gems than Dale Winton's bathroom. At least I was old enough to miss hearing Mass in Latin. In my parents' day the Church believed so much in the mystery of God they revealed it in a language no one could understand. If you wanted to know how much Jesus loved you, you had to take along Linguaphone tapes.

The depressing thing about religious people is their sheer bloody-mindedness. A Christian coalition recently organised an advertising campaign to be shown on the side of buses in response to an atheist campaign. Personally, I'm in favour of any religious war carried out on buses that doesn't involve blowing me up. If people aren't swayed by the Pope, the Bible, the Koran, Jesus and four thousand years of organised religion, I'm not sure the number 16 to Larkhall is going to cut it. The message reads,

'There definitely is a God.' Yeah, tell that to the poor sod who drives the bus and gets spat on ten times a day for the minimum wage. It might be more accurate if the message was printed on the inside of the bus and read, 'There definitely is a God. And he hates you.'

I have a theory about the Pope. You know how he fought for the Nazis? Well if Nazi scientists did manage to save Hitler's brain then maybe they kept it alive in a jar for years waiting to implant it into someone with power on the world stage. That someone would need to wear a very big hat to hide all the stitching left by a brain transplant. They probably thought about putting his brain into an NFL quarterback but held out for the Pope. The Pope has said that condoms don't help prevent the spread of AIDS. Someone ought to tell His Holiness that he must be putting them on wrong. You'd have though the Pope would have been well up for using condoms. It would have scuppered the court cases of many of his priests if there was no DNA evidence. In Africa AIDS has killed 25 million people in three decades. That's a lot of funerals. I can see why the Pope doesn't want to lose the work.

There was a thing at primary called 'The Black Babies'. It was a hugely misguided charitable effort they used to drop on us in Catholic schools. You sponsored an African baby and, I think, sometimes got to name them. At least, that's what I'm told by my African friends Wolf Tone and Murdo McCloud. Anyway, there was always some daft kid who misunderstood and thought that they'd actually get the baby for a bit. They were too young to realise that there are a thousand good reasons why a little African baby shouldn't be shipped off to another country and that human beings should never be exchanged for money. I think that Madonna basically has the emotional development of one of those kids. She can pay for a little black baby, so why shouldn't she get to keep it? She's probably been drawn in by the advertising – if you get an African kid it costs £2 a month to feed and if it gets cataracts they're only a pound to fix. Actually, I feel really sorry for little David Banda. The only black role models he'll have growing up will be homosexual backing dancers. Madonna is said to have had his nursery painted like a jungle, to make him feel at home. Hopefully the kitchen's done out like the inside of a UN helicopter.

Every summer we went to stay at my gran's place in Ireland. She lived in a really remote part of Donegal, which is beautiful and bleak. I'd say maybe a little of the bleakness seeps into the people. The bit we lived in wasn't so much quiet as empty. If someone wanted to film a movie there that was set after a nuclear apocalypse they would have had to bus people in.

My gran lived with my granddad, my great-uncle and my uncle James in a little whitewashed farmhouse. My brother and I would sleep in a small room with both uncles, my great-uncle often getting himself off to sleep with a long, tongue-in-cheek monologue about how we were going to Hell, and listing all the torments that would be waiting for us. I always enjoyed it as a sort of grim joke, but it worried John and afterwards you could hear him muttering his prayers hard even over all the snoring.

They were all very religious. My uncle got a new car and nobody would get into it until a priest had been out to bless the thing. A priest came out and got paid to tell the story of the Good Samaritan and throw holy water over the bonnet. My granny prayed a lot, for everybody. I sometimes wonder if I'm not still just working through the goodwill she built up with for me with God. One day soon I'm going to run out of her Hail Marys and both my legs will drop off.

Everybody was obsessed with death in that household. They'd talk about it a lot. Once we were all getting on the bus as we left at the end of summer and I said 'See you next year!' to my granddad. 'I'll be dead next year,' he replied, without sadness. That's Catholicism; it's a great big death cult. Look around a church at all the golden crucifixes, the big marble statues of Jesus dying. The nativity, the only part of the story that's about life, is just a temporary thing they throw up for a few weeks. It's generally focussed round a £5.99 Tiny Tears doll – one year our church had a rocking horse for the donkey. It had 'I'm a cowboy' written on it.

My granddad was a difficult guy. Joyless, to the point where he found other people's laughter upsetting. He'd often scold us for laughing, as would my mum. They thought that laughter was infantile. I thought the idea of somebody hating children's laughter was really funny, like an ogre in a fairytale. My granddad had a very hard life. He grew up in poverty I can't imagine at a time when children were hired out to farms as rural labour. He had to work in Scotland to support his brothers and sisters, and ended up burying most of them when they were still young. Now his health was gone and he was in constant pain. I knew all this, but I was a child so I hated him for being a grumpy old cunt.

Boredom was a huge part of our lives there. It's the rainiest county in Ireland. Which is a bit like saying you're the Dirtiest Woman in Dundee – a lot of competition and little prestige. Often we'd be stuck indoors listening to fiddle music on a crackling radio. Everybody spoke Irish so you'd have to entertain yourself. I read loads of books there on my top bunk, the days ticking by slowly. I'd always run out of actual kids' books and have to dive into my granddad's stack of masculine adventure novels. There was a real lurch trying to get into a story of a mercenary on the run from the East German police when you'd just finished a book about a boy who had magic shoes.

They farmed sheep there and occasionally we'd have to help out, acting as auxiliary sheepdogs when the sheep were being herded, or taking lunch out to the shearers when they clipped them in a nearby pit. There were actual dogs as well and we'd be so bored we'd dote on them to a degree they found exasperating. These creatures had to have a complex skillset – able to run after sheep on a hill but also to put up with little children who wanted to make them wear a blouse.

The highlight of every week was the arrival of the baker's van. This guy drove around the middle of nowhere selling cakes and sweets and stuff, and we would clean him out. We'd be sitting on rocks with nothing but fields for miles eating these bright purple or luminous yellow cakes. Every Sunday a wee bus came to take everybody to Mass in the local town of Dungloe. Mass was crushingly dull and sometimes in Irish, but afterwards you were in town till the bus left. A proper town with sweets and penknives and toy guns and footballs.

Dungloe was famous in Ireland for its annual summer beauty contest called 'Mary from Dungloe'. Irish communities from all over the globe would contribute fresh and conventional-looking examples of their gene pool. You'd have a Chicago Mary and a Glasgow Mary; who knows what their real names were? The whole thing was exactly like Father Ted's 'Lovely Girl's Contest' and everyone for miles around seemed obsessed with the thing. One year a local girl won – Moia McCole, the Donegal Mary. She lived at the bottom of our hill and everybody was really excited. They drove about at night honking on their car horns and there were big bonfires and parties. The *Sunday World* printed a photo of her where she was leaning forward a little too far and you could see her nipple. I cut it out and had a wank behind a big rock.

There was a peculiarity in that part of the world whereby people sometimes had a second name related to their job. I guess it started because so many people had the same first names and surnames. The guy who delivered the post was Dimrick the Post. There was a baker in Dungloe who my mum's family knew as Anthony the Cake, but my dad's lot called Anthony the Bun. It was great meeting people who were called the Van or the Loaf. It was like a whimsical branch of American wrestling.

Often we'd get driven to the pub by my uncle where we'd drink something called 'Football Special' in life-threatening quantities. We particularly loved it because it had a head on it like a pint of beer. Looking back it was actually a thick chemical scum. It also meant that we were basically drunk on sugar.

The main pub we went to was called Tessie's. It was a run-down place with a stone floor and barrels in the corner. On cold nights you all sat in Tessie's kitchen by the fire. Everybody played a card game called '25' for tiny stakes – fifty pences was about the limit. In reality it was just an excuse for people to curse each other and the games were always accompanied by explosions of laughter. They'd curse each other for playing their hand badly or too well, for winning too much or being a sore loser or a cheap bastard or just a bastard. One time some American tourists wandered in and asked if they sold low-alcohol lager – they asked half a dozen drunks playing cards on a barrel as a dog ate crisps off the floor. After a disbelieving pause everybody screamed with laughter. This wasn't just rudeness; nobody there had heard of such a thing as low-alcohol lager and it sounded like a ridiculous contradiction.

We kids loved going to the pub and would get really upset on the nights the men would go without us. It's possible that we were cripplingly addicted to the sugar high. Some nights we'd go to bed then hear the car leaving the drive, so we'd run out after them. We knew we couldn't stop them going without us. I think we just wanted to leave them with the image of us in their rear mirror, standing in the doorway in our pyjamas forming a tableau of disappointment and recrimination.

There was a relaxed attitude to drink-driving, in that you were basically allowed to drink-drive. I saw a guy one night struggle to get his key into the car door for a few minutes then hop in and drive off. My uncle would have about ten pints some nights and then drive us all home. I guess the feeling was that we weren't going to crash into anyone, because barely any fucker lived there.

One year I went over to Ireland with my mum in winter. It was really beautiful in the snow. My cousin Mark was there too and every morning we'd pull our wellies on and walk for miles in a different direction, always finding somewhere interesting. I think it's my memory of this period that makes me fantasise about living in the country. In reality I know there would be no shops and I would kill myself.

I was generally pretty bored and under-stimulated when I was a little kid. Other than going out to play in the backs, we didn't really do much of anything. My brother and I got a Spectrum computer one Christmas and it totally took over our lives for a couple of years. There were loads of addictive games which to a modern child would seem like playing with a jobbie on a stick. It's amazing what people were doing with less memory than is currently in the average vibrator. Those games were like little coding haikus. There was one called *Schooldaze*, which was a chillingly realistic depiction of school. You had wee tasks to do for your own benefit but everything got derailed because you had to spend all of your time in classes or you'd get punished. I intensified the reality loop by sometimes failing to do my homework because I was playing the game. There were some surprising freedoms in it too. You could, for example, just fuck yourself out of the top-floor window and fall to your death. The Headmaster would stand over your corpse and say, 'You are not a bird, Eric', quite callously I thought. Also you could go into the empty rooms and write swearwords on the blackboards, which we thought was unbelievably hilarious. The teacher would give you lines if they actually caught you but seemed remarkably calm about teaching a class who were looking at the word 'Cuntbucket'.

There was also a game called *Emlyn Hughes's Supersoccer*. Like everybody, we hated Emlyn Hughes but the game was strangely compelling. There was a bug where if you put a heavy tackle in on someone they would just sort of die – lie down on the pitch and just never get up. Their inert form would be repositioned by the computer for free-kicks. You could also score from a kick-off by taking a really big run-up and just blooter it into your opponent's goal. My brother and I had a tensely negotiated agreement not to do this and we both did it absolutely every time.

I was about eleven when I started going to the cinema by myself; my parents just had no interest in that kind of thing. I really wanted to see *Star Wars* because everybody at school had the action figures and was talking about *Return of the Jedi*. Eventually my dad said he'd take me. What he actually took me to was the first *Star Trek* movie, the really shit one with the baldy woman in it. I've never had the heart to tell him.

The first thing I went to see on my own was *Footloose*. I was really into old rock and roll records and thought it sounded brilliant. I borrowed my brother's fake leather jacket and sat in the cinema with the collar turned up. It's still pretty weird that those guys were Kevin Bacon and Chris Penn, and that it was basically gay.

I started taking my sister along to the local cinema in Muirend, a real time capsule with staff who looked like they were being hunted by Ghostbusters. There was a doorman called Frank. Strictly speaking, what he was actually called was 'Frank the Wank', something people shouted at him everywhere he went. I was on a bus years later and two teenagers saw him coming out of a newsagent in his civvies and actually got off the bus to shout it at him. I'd drag my sister along to my choice of movies – which meant every rubbish fantasy film that came out, things like *Krull* and *Beastmaster*. I think my parents would give me the ticket money for both of us if I took her along, so I'd bribe her with Maltesers and she'd sit there dispassionately watching Rutger Hauer have an unconvincing swordfight with a man dressed as a cyclops.

I was really excited when the old cartoon version of *The Lord of the Rings* got a showing at the GFT. As a kid I'd have been delighted to know that everybody would eventually get into

Tolkien. This is back in the days when fantasy was just for total nerds. There were about a dozen to fifteen heavily bespectacled kids – one was a diabetic whose mum had brought him a big box of raisins for a snack. It was great to set eyes on Glasgow's other dweebs. There was a bit when Aragorn laid into some orcs and we just all went mental. I think life is a lot different for alternative kids nowadays. Texting and the internet mean that being a Goth or something means you're part of a big social scene, it's an inclusive thing. Back then, we all just went our different ways in the afterglow, wishing each other all the best with the next ten years of bullying.

THREE

I know one shouldn't dwell on the past, so I've really tried to put the misery of my secondary education behind me. On the other hand, if I ever meet Steven Tilsbury again, I'm going to bundle him into the back of a campervan, which I've had specially adapted by the Chinese military, and he's going to spend a very difficult nine months strapped to a surgical table, fed intravenously, while I create a masterpiece of suffering with a nail file and a cigarette lighter. STEAL MY FOOTBALL SOCKS WILL YOU STEVEN?

School days are only happy if you have a particular yen to be taught five hours of geography a week by a convicted paedophile. Actually, to be serious, the sex at school was embarrassing. You'd think after 20 years the janitor would know what he's doing. I still can't come unless I'm in a small dark room filled with sports equipment.

There's that amazing cliché that schooldays are the best days of your life. Things have gone very wrong in your life if your best days involved being shouted at by an alcoholic for spelling 'broccoli' with two i's. Anyone who had the best time of their life at school has never licked LSD off what they think used to be a hooker. To be fair I didn't hate everything about school. I only hated the teachers, the pupils, the lessons, the building, the food, the smell, every second I spent there – but I have to say the drive-way was sort of OK.

The journey to secondary school involved taking a bus and then walking for a couple of miles. The walk always had the sun hanging directly in front of me – the Mayans couldn't have aligned this thing any more directly with the fucking sun. When it had been raining there would be puddles reflecting the light up into your eyes and it felt like walking into the belly of a spacecraft.

Our school was a zoo for children. On my first day I sat shell-shocked at the side of the playground, a complex ballet of dead-arms, gambling, taunts and violence. At one end were railings surrounding a deep staircase into the basement. This was the 'grog pit'. If someone's bag could be got off them it would be hurled down these steps. If they went down to fetch it, an animal howl of 'GROG PIT!' would go up and the whole school would crowd up onto the railings and spit on them. I saw a tiny first year emerge to jeers, wet and slippery like a newborn calf. I instantly knew that my task for the next five years was to get through this.

Later I found that a big part of surviving was to get yourself a lockable room in which you could sit out lunchtime. Teachers would sometimes give the keys to their classroom to responsible kids, ostensibly to do work. It was actually so these weaker spec-imens could have a locked door between them and those who wanted to take their money, humiliate them or simply punch them repeatedly in the arms and legs. I was in the Latin Club and half a dozen of us would have lunch there for a couple of years. I'd never studied Latin, and could probably have survived in General Population. Michelle Caldwell was in the Latin Club though, and she tended to cross her legs in a way that let you see up her skirt. I loved Latin Club.

I should probably mention here that the Latin teacher who let us have the room was a nice chap who was the school's expert on sex education. A spindly, balding man with a ginger homeless beard, he'd occasionally pop up into religious classes and give a lecture on contraception. Apparently the only thing that was allowed was something called the rhythm method, but withdrawal was preferable to, eh, using a condom. I imagined that he practised withdrawal a wee bit himself as he had a noticeable facial twitch. Almost a spasm, it made him look as if he was about to yell out some obscene prophecy. He had nine children.

Even having a room didn't guarantee safety as often crowds would gather round them like zombies, trying to break in or holding the door closed after the bell so everybody inside would be late for their next class. A guy tried to break into the Latin room one time through one of those little strips at the top of a window, the kind you have to undo with a hook on a stick. He was an enormous, powerful guy – unbelievably tall. I knew his family and they had contacted *The Guinness Book of Records* because they were convinced that he had the biggest feet of any boy his age in the world. I also knew he was adopted. Who knows how his adoptive parents must have felt as this enormous, villainous cuckoo grew to dwarf them in their home? It was a tense lunchtime, two of us trying to stop the door from being kicked in, the others trying to push these record-breaking feet back out through the window.

There was a lot of behaviour from the kids that just verged on madness. On our first day in technical class we got this long lecture about safety in the classroom. We were all just looking at each other in disbelief thinking, 'No way! They're giving us chisels?' Within seconds of the talk finishing someone blew metal filings into somebody else's eyes and that was that – a year of technical drawing instead.

One of the technical teachers had a bizarre burbling voice. He was a bit like an incomprehensible version of Bernie Winters. Once he gave me a long talking to and I had genuinely no idea if it was praise or censure. Probably the latter, as I was pish at techie. There was an assignment to build a little bookcase once. I didn't have a clue so I stole the display model that the teacher had done. Just so it wasn't too obvious I re-glued the runners on the bottom and ended up with a C.

The technical classes back then were idiotic. Teenage kids are like the A-Team. Give them a few rudimentary objects and they'll construct a death machine of some kind. By the end of term the class was more tooled up than an Orc army. It's like a conspiracy. Why don't they teach kids in poor areas how to be hedge-fund managers and bond traders? Instead they get shown how to make mug trees and spice racks.

Years later I was writing on *8 out of 10 Cats*, working on their *Big Brother* special. I'd watched *Big Brother* all that week to get up to speed and was pretty horrified.

'They must really sift through the applicants to find such fuck-ing idiots!' I groaned. 'I mean, people aren't all just fucking idiots are they?'

Jimmy Carr just looked at me patiently and said, 'Don't you remember school?' I suppose that's true, the place was full of utter goobers. Once we were doing a science experiment in pairs. It was about velocity, so you measured how fast a little car went down a slope with five weights on it, then four and so on, to see if mass affected velocity. I was paired with a big, dotie *Of Mice and Men* character. I set the car with five weights and went to put it at the start line. He took it from me and ripped three of the weights off. 'No point using five!' he scoffed. 'There's only fuck-ing two of us.'

Some of my favourite kids at school were the pathological liars. It seems that a tiny but indefatigable percentage of any school population will claim their bones have been replaced with metal and that they hang out with U2. The best one I knew was a boy called Ed Raven. He transferred into our school in second year but looked about eighteen and was sort of a hunchback. He claimed to have been living in Germany, where he was the national BMX champion. He also said he was independently wealthy, owning a meat factory near Berlin. I mean, if you could lie about anything, who would lay claim to a meat factory? Ed Raven would. That was his genius. My friend bumped into him many years later outside Glasgow Uni. Raven was walking with a cane and brushed past him having no time to answer questions. His ship was moored in the Clyde and he had to get back before the crew grew restive.

There was another guy like that in one of my classes. He came in late one day and started into some crazy excuse. We all perked up because we knew that somewhere in the explanation he was going to be mauled by a leopard or something. The teacher cut into what he was saying and made him tell the actual story of why he was late and it was … his mum making him wait in for the gasman. You could see a real look on his face that said, 'What's the point of telling you this? This is boring.' I think that was the thing with those kids, they thought that our reality was so boring it literally wasn't worth living in. They were sort of right, too.

Apparently parents tell an average of 3,000 white lies to children while they are growing up. My parents told me that every time you told a lie a giant fire-breathing spider with the head of a bear and the arms of an octopus would spin a big web out of all your lies and then when it had spun a web big enough it would carry you off in it. Of course it wasn't until years later I found out they had been lying to me all along and they weren't my real parents. Personally, I'm looking forward to telling my kids they were adopted. They weren't, I'm just looking forward to telling them that.

I had friends but kept myself apart from most people, largely because I felt that they were all heading for grim jobs and Barratt houses in an unquestioning way that I found alarming. Still, there was always a part of me that wondered if I should try to be part of the gang more and forget about my doubts. I just couldn't imagine being part of that world though, having a job, a mortgage, marrying your girlfriend from school and sending your own kids back there. Thing is, I've met a lot of people from school since and they've done all that, done the stuff I only used to say they'd do as a sort of despairing joke.

In my late twenties I was out with my best friend Paul Marsh (Paul is a transcendent human being and full-scale nutcase who I will colour in lovingly later on). I've known Paul since school and he's flowered into a real independent thinker. On this occasion he was wearing a green leather jacket and some kind of tartan bondage trousers. I'd been writing all day on ecstasy. A guy came up to us who'd been at school with us both; he had a little pot belly and greying temples and was wearing the same windcheater my dad has. Now I'm not saying he's a bad guy; he's actually a lovely guy, but he looked at Paul dressed as some kind of Space Clown and me looking like I was trying to stare through the fabric of the universe and he said, 'So lads! Are you getting much golf in?'

There was quite a telling thing that happened right at the start of my second year. There was an open patio area that linked different parts of the school. A bunch of us were dawdling through there and suddenly a big group just attacked this guy called John Jo. I think he'd literally looked at somebody in the wrong way – suddenly a group was round him punching and kicking him with one big lad slamming his head off a wall. John Jo just never came back; his mum took him out of the school. I remember our form teacher giving us a sarcastic speech about how his mum had come up to the school and said he wouldn't be back. The form teacher was utterly incredulous that someone would transfer out because he'd been subjected to a serious, unprovoked assault. His point was pretty explicit – if she didn't like her son's head getting rattled off a wall, she'd struggle to find anywhere she'd like in the Glasgow school system.

It wasn't the roughest school in Glasgow, nowhere close to it, but it would probably have shocked a lot of people. Quite a few people I knew there are dead now. A wee guy called Billy Kerr got killed by his dad, who chopped his head off in a drunken rage. His old man was a butcher, so at least he'd have made a good job of it. The guy who told me he'd been killed added brutally, '… not so wide anymore'. 'Probably not quite as tall as he used to be either …,' I sighed.

There was a nearby school that was some kind of special institution. I don't know quite what it was, a List D school, borstal or some kind of learning difficulties place. Anyway, anyone you met from there was either a hardcore villain or mentally handi-capped. One lunchtime a whole crew of them turned up at our school, smashing windows and battering people. It was like a fucking Zulu movie. A big group gathered outside one of the entrances – I think they had a beef with somebody in particular and were calling him out. One of our teachers (a hard case) walked out calmly and headbutted the biggest one right to the ground. It was like Clint Eastwood. Or like a grown man head-butting an emotionally troubled boy. It was tremendous.

Of course, life then was probably less violent than it is for the average teenager nowadays. I certainly think that teenagers should be taught more about knife crime. Going for the kidneys can give you a much cleaner kill. Equally, news footage of the teenage victims of gun crime should teach us all something. Look closely at those notes left by friends as the cameras pan by – there is a lesson to be learned here. These kids just can't spell. 'Respek'? What's that? They certainly won't be getting any of my respect until they learn some basic spelling and punctuation. Modern youth also seem to be horrible gift buyers. Do you really think this guy would have appreciated a teddy bear? He was a crack dealer!

Our diets at school were laughably terrible. Loads of us would go for chips at lunch – chips and a potato fritter was the top seller. That's a bag of chips and an enormous chip please. My mum would make me a packed lunch, so I'd spend a fair bit of time trying to barter gammon rolls and Blue Ribband biscuits into something more interesting. There was an ice-cream van outside the front gates that sold single fags and a tuck shop that only seemed to sell choc-ices. I loved it and I'd have appreciated it all even more if I could see myself now – forcing myself to eat a bowl of leaves with my meals in a desperate attempt to stay alive.

I do think kids need better education about nutrition – I didn't really have a clue about any of that stuff till I read up on it a few years ago. Scientists have found that people who choose to eat crisps, chips and chocolate have a gene linked to obesity. They are now able to identify the group of people with this gene, by looking at a map of Scotland. Apparently, the SNP is to give every schoolchild in Scotland an obesity check. If they can't fit into one of Alex Salmond's trouser legs they go on a diet.

One of the fattest boys at my school was called Jerry MacBrayne. There was a rumour that he'd been caught masturbating during chemistry class. Nobody knew if it was true, but we all abused him about it endlessly because there wasn't much else to do. He had these really fat parents, a fat sister and a wee fat dog. They'd all go jogging together in a nearby park in terry towelling tracksuits. My friend, a mischievous wee lassie called Lesley, lived across from them. She phoned a curry house one night and sent them half the menu as a prank. She said his dad answered the door and looked absolutely delighted.

The idea has been floated that parents of obese children should be fined. Don't people realise that the parents of fat children are simply misguided? What they're trying to do is make their kids less attractive to paedophiles. What they're forgetting is that they're making it more difficult for them to run away. In Vegas I once saw an incredibly fat man on one of those little mobility scooter things, except he'd driven it onto a moving walkway, so he didn't even have to drive. Now that's lazy.

Live Aid was a huge thing at school. I think it's fair enough for kids to get excited about something like that. But the adults who bought it should have really been embarrassed. 'The Christmas bells that ring there are … the clanging chimes of doom?' Did that really happen? Even at 12, I'd had a host of sexual night-mares that were less weird than the video to that song. If there's one thing we've learned about fighting famine over the years it is this – big music events don't work. We can tick that off the list. To be honest, you'd have thought that would have been a bit further down the list. It's amazing to think that at some point there was a meeting where someone said, 'People are starving in their millions', and somebody replied, 'We'd better get a hold of Ultravox and Annie Lennox.'

Seeing the film *Gandhi* was also a massive thing for me as a kid. I saw a clip of it on TV first, where Gandhi as a young man is thrown off a train because of his race. I just felt this incredible indignation that stuff like that happened in the world. I talked to my dad about it and was absolutely raging. I suppose that was the birth of some kind of political consciousness. Apparently the London Underground is using quotes from *Gandhi* on the Tube. But I don't remember his saying, 'There's a body on the line at Marble Arch' in the film. They are using other famous quotes too, but the one from the Koran emptied the train.

I was quite into socialism and read stuff like *The Ragged Trousered Philanthropists* and George Orwell. I was quite an idealistic wee boy and I'd read quite a lot of political stuff by the time I was about 14. By 16 I joined the Labour Party. That didn't seem like such a great place for an idealist. Or anyone with a low boredom threshold. It's a rarely mentioned fact that politicians rise through the ranks by being able to sit through endless grim meetings. This inevitably means that we are governed by monsters. A few months of screaming inwardly during speeches about council business and I drifted off. It's not like our political system even gets stuff done. Motorists now have to dodge a pothole for every 120 yards of road in Britain. It's estimated it will take 13 years and cost £1 billion before council workers will finish standing around staring at all of them.

Politicians are just innately ridiculous and their lives can't really bear the weight of much scrutiny. As a teenager I campaigned for Labour in a Glasgow by-election. The candidate was Mike Watson, who seemed like a reasonably genuine, socialist-minded character. He was elected, forgot about the socialism and later became Lord Watson. When I heard that he'd tried to burn down a hotel at the Scottish Politician of the Year Awards I assumed that he'd had a change of heart. Mike must have had an epiphany, I reasoned, surrounded by these braying crooks at their annual backslapper. Realising what he had done with his life he must have tried to bring the whole place down about their heads like a modern-day Samson! I did a gig at that hotel recently and the staff told me that he'd started the fire because they'd stopped serving him at the bar. My dad always had a generally socialist outlook. His philosophy was a strange mixture of apathy and class war. He didn't want to smash the state but he wished that someone would. The good thing was that he would talk to us about stuff like that and we had an idea that the world might be a bit different from what we saw on the news. Once, my headmistress held a discussion about nuclear war, a subject I had questioned people endlessly about due to fear.

'Did you know that there are underground bunkers where key people will go when there's a nuclear alert?' she asked the generally baffled class.

'Yes Miss! My dad says that all the top politicians will go there.'

'That's right Frankie, a lot of key people will be taken there, so that the country will be able to keep running.'

'Dad said that if he knew where one was, he'd get a shotgun when the four-minute warning went off and shoot everybody as they went in!'

My music teacher stood in a Glasgow by-election. He was a foaming Nationalist and once demonstrated the battle tactics at Culloden to us using a clipboard (shield) and pen (sword). He got a party political broadcast, which he sung. We all rushed home to see it.

'Oh, these are my mountains!' he cried, gesturing at some tower blocks. 'And this is my glen!' He was pointing into a local canal, full of rubbish. It was fantastic.

There were pupils who struggled to get through life at school but it was the same for some of the teachers. There was a maths teacher called Mr Hughes: an unfortunately camp heterosexual who for some reason chose to wear shoes with little golden buckles. Everywhere he went kids sang 'Mr Hughes, the Elephant Man' to the tune of 'Over the Hills and Far Away'. He was a lightning rod for spitballs, paper aeroplanes and any kind of improvised missile.

There was a game where kids would inch their tables forward when the teacher turned to write something on the blackboard. Mr Hughes just didn't have the personal confidence to address it, so we'd all end up crowded round his legs. Sometimes his face would be pressed up against the board. One time he made a joke.

'What would you measure a waistline in, centimetres or metres or kilometres?' he asked.

'Metres', said Harriet Adams, a reputedly slack lassie, being deliberately unhelpful.

'I suppose it might be measured in metres if you were Cyril Smith,' quipped Mr Hughes, chortling at his own joke.

We all laughed too, and kept laughing. There was an instant telepathic understanding that we were never going to stop. People outdid each other trying to laugh the loudest, the most gratingly, screaming like animals until it started to become genuinely hilarious. Tears were running down faces and people were gasping for air, shrieking. A boy clawed at his throat like he was going to suffocate. Mr Hughes stood entirely passive throughout, staring not at but through the back wall.

Mr Hughes decided that teaching was not for him and left to become a bus driver. Fate is cruel and his route took him directly by the school. People would run out in their lunchtime to the bus-stop and sing the 'Elephant Man' song at him when he opened the doors, waving their arms up against their faces like trunks.

Our science teacher was called Mr Clarkson. He was always drunk and would drop things on the floor so he could try to look up the girls' skirts. Every week he gave a mumbling, incoherent lecture called 'The Life of a Battery'. It didn't appear anywhere on the syllabus and even with repetition nobody was ever able to piece together exactly what it was he was saying.

Remember that old joke about the Pope needing a heart transplant? He drops a feather from his balcony and whoever it lands on has to give the Pope his heart. When he looks down he sees thousands of people all blowing desperately. Well, Clarkson had a version of that. If the class grew restless while he rubbed out and redrew his battery diagram he would decide that somebody was getting a 'punishment exercise'. He'd push a piece of paper down one of those big, long science tables and whoever it stopped at would take the punishment. Of course we all blew like fuck. I remember seeing a mum up at the school complaining about the number of undeserved punishments her son kept getting, not realising it was because he was an asthmatic.

PE was generally dreaded. The teachers seemed to occupy something of an educational hinterland. Nominally a teacher but actually just a guy who likes running and throwing stuff. They were obsessed with getting us to climb ropes and wall-bars, like they were preparing us for a career in the eighteenth-century merchant navy. Our main teacher was a fitness nut called Mr McKean. At our first lesson he gave us a long speech about how flexibility peaked at twelve and explained that we were all stiffening towards death. Then we played dodgeball.

We had an annual football event where everybody played a class that was a year older. It was notorious for its brutality and warming up there was the testosterone level of a botched prison break. I waited for the opening whistle and ran straight at the smallest guy on the other team and hoofed him right in the balls. I had to do laps for an hour but the scene I was running round looked like a kung fu tribute to *Saving Private Ryan*.

In second year there was a big formal run that everybody dreaded. Five miles round a big cinder-ash marsh. I came 123rd out of 132 boys. The fattest boy in the school was a guy called Chris Katos, whose dad ran a kebab shop. On the second lap I spotted him hiding under a bush at the side of the track, eating an enormous bag of pakora. It was like something from *The Dandy*.

Our drama class was taken by Miss Skillen – a little middle-aged woman with huge tits forming an obscene shelf at right angles to her body. Occasionally producers would come into the school and host auditions for parts in TV dramas. They can't all have been like this, but the ones I went to always had English producers looking for people to play stereotypical heavy Glaswegians. I remember they were casting somebody to play a drug dealer and there was an audition piece where boys had to shake down a smaller boy for money. Everybody loved this one guy, who delivered a performance of some gusto. He got something like five grand for the film and went on to enjoy a two-year-long party.

Even among the kids who did the auditions, there was an amused awareness of being stereotyped. If Sir Ian McKellen had been born in Glasgow right now he'd be playing a glue-sniffing bouncer with bi-polar disorder. We're our own worst enemy. Even programmes made in Scotland portray most Scots as loveable chancers on heroin and incapacity benefit. Imagine if every TV show from America was about a cowboy eating hot dogs on the electric chair. Just once I'd love to see a sitcom based on Dundonian transgender ballet dancers living on a barge.

I couldn't act at all but I got a couple of parts as an extra with a line or two. I was a cheeky young gardener in a *Play for Today*. There was a bit where a bunch of us were supposed to shout abuse at Russell Hunter, who was the star, as we walked by in the distance. I couldn't think of anything else to say so I just shouted 'Clitoris!' over and over again. You could hear it quite clearly when it went out on telly. I think the producers just couldn't understand my accent but it baffled a lot of viewers in Scotland.

Later, I was a cheeky milkboy in an episode of *Dramarama*, starring Mark McManus. Taggart! He slept in his dressing room quite a bit and would occasionally stumble into mine in a dressing gown and ask if I had any fags. There was none of the tedium an adult would associate with being an extra. I was getting paid to be off school. It was like finding the cheat codes for the universe.

Kids had to have chaperones on set, so I got to meet some interesting characters. One woman I had was an adorable 50-something Glasgow mum. She would go on about her passion for Richard Chamberlain ('a waste of a good man') and generally gossiped at me like I was cutting her hair. My favourite was this moustachioed socialist guy who would discourse on what he'd do to various politicians and celebrities if he got them alone in a room. If you're stuck in a Portakabin for long enough with anyone – even a young kid – you'll eventually just start being yourself. His marriage, he confided, had been in trouble because of his libido, but had been greatly strengthened by the arrival of AIDS, which stopped him wanting other women.

'Used to be a pretty girl would smile at me and I wouldn't be home for three days. You caught anything, the doctor gave you a jab and told you not to drink for a while. Not any more. The party's over.'

I loved people talking to me like an equal. I was always sad when the job was finished and I had to leave the stories and the card games and the bacon rolls. Looking back, that was the start of my interest in show business. I didn't particularly enjoy the performing but I did love the camaraderie and the sheer variety of folk, endlessly talking shit.

The school had an annual talent show, which my best friend Craig and I did one year with a filthy act of pretty basic sex material. We were two detectives, talking about our cases as being a bit of a side issue to all the women we'd fucked. It wasn't even really double entendre; there was clearly only one way you could take it and everybody was horrified. After that they'd make us audition every year for the talent show on our own, and then ban us. I used to look forward to the wee audition, just standing on our own in an empty lecture theatre doing blue jokes to our very elderly deputy head's flinty, unchanging scowl.

The shows were always compered by two good-looking drama monkeys called Victor and Andy. Their schtick was that one would come on and say, 'Where's Andy?' then go off to look for him while the other came on and went, 'Where's Victor.' I hated those guys and, denied any other role in the show, we'd go and heckle them. I'd like to say it was witty heckling; it wasn't.

'Where's Andy?'

'You're a CUNT, Victor!'

We did notice that people in the drama society seemed to be fucking each other. I guess that's the way of the acting profession everywhere and I salute it. We even thought about getting involved, purely for sexual reasons. I went to a school production of *Guys and Dolls* as a reconnaissance exercise and decided it wasn't worth it. There was a girl who was the school's Sharpay, who was a hirsute lassie routinely referred to as Teenwolf. She had these really hairy arms and kind of lady sideburns. All the guys affected to dislike her but we were all secretly turned on by the fact that she was a known shagger and must have had a muff like Henry Cooper's armpit.

There was a thing I got into the habit of doing that was basically the start of my comedy career. There were two attractive girls in the debating society and I knew the entrance they used to come into school. I'd hang around there most days, trying to look like I'd just turned up for school early and hung around near the gates without going in, like a lunatic. Each time I would have some little stories and jokes and stuff that I'd go over in my head on the way to school. It wasn't that I thought I could get anywhere with them – they were a couple of years older and one of them was dating a huge and disturbing Chinese guy who worked as a bouncer. It was more that making women laugh was pretty much all they'd let me do to them – so I really threw myself into it.

I was always able to make people laugh. In fact I remember at school being able to make them laugh really hard. Imagine nowadays if you were only happy with your gig if you'd made someone spit their drink out, or made milk shoot out of their nose. If a joke worked with one girl I'd keep it and maybe add something for the next one – working a little bit like a real comedian and driven by horniness. Actually, exactly like a real comedian.

I was really into *The Comic Strip Presents* when it was on Channel 4 and *Saturday Night Live*. I seemed to be the only person in school who watched any of that stuff. It's easy to forget that while alternative comedy is now the mainstream, at the time it was a real minority interest.

It was watching Ben Elton that first made me aware of green issues. People give him a lot of stick now because he wrote some Queen musical that causes cancer, but I think he did a really good job of introducing green politics to a generation. Also, he wrote *Blackadder*, so he could write a musical about Ian Huntley and he'd still be alright by me. I'm always amazed that people aren't more horrified by things like the ice caps melting. To me it feels like living in a nightmare. It's just as well Scott of the Antarctic wasn't setting off nowadays. It'd be a pretty boring journal. 'Day 1. Got there. Day 2. Came home. Went to pub.' Now if you get to the South Pole you can bring it home in a flask.

As soon as the sun comes out we are faced with the usual tabloid headlines about scorching weather. Wouldn't it be great for a tabloid front page to cover hot weather with a picture of a girl in a bikini with the headline 'Global Warming Forces Desperate Polar Bears to Eat Each Other'? Changing weather patterns mean that animals are going to start to migrate differently. Personally I look forward to seeing Bill Oddie going to do some birdwatching in Norfolk and getting his head ripped off by a puma.

I'm not sure I trust science to get us out of this mess. We tend to put all our faith in science these days. Scientists are planning to build a vault on the moon that contains details of crop growing and instructions for metal smelting so that survivors of a nuclear war or an asteroid collision could restart civilisation. There's just one small problem I see with this plan – how are a ragtag band of survivors meant to access a vault on the fucking moon? I already have a detailed plan of action for coping with global warming when it really starts to affect Scotland. I'm going to remove a couple of jumpers.

Actually, I think the most sensible thing to do to find out how the planet is going is to have a friend who's a scientist. When he takes up smoking it's time to worry. Or when he suddenly goes for a visit to the moon with all of his scientist friends.

'Just going for the weekend, John? You seem to be taking a lot of canned goods ...?'

I'd say my overall outlook for the future is pessimistic. Here's a theory of mine. You know how years ago David Bowie used to always be slightly ahead of the curve? He covered the Velvet Underground just before people heard of them, and seemed to be riding each new wave of the zeitgeist? Even *Tin Machine* could be seen as him trying to do grunge slightly too early. Well, my theory is the government captured Bowie and replaced him with a lookalike. They keep the real Bowie in a big glass prison room, like Hannibal Lecter, so they can observe him and predict future trends. I reckon everybody is shitting themselves because recently Bowie developed metal skin and turned Chinese.

The fact there were pretty girls in the debating society convinced me to join and I loved it. In it, the hideous flaws in my personality suddenly turned into virtues. I looked at the debating society in the way that a bank robber looks at an easy score, trying to spot the catch. I was a facetious, argumentative bastard and it turned out that it was a game that required you to be a facetious, argumentative bastard. The only other boys looked like even bigger losers than me. It just seemed too perfect.

The woman who ran the debating society was called Pat Slaven. She is a truly wonderful woman and if I ever invent a time machine I will go back in time and marry her. Right after I've finished fucking the young Diana Rigg.

I took the whole thing really seriously, as I honestly saw it as a chance to impress girls. Yes, I saw what is now clearly the club least attractive to women as a chance to impress girls. How many people have lost their virginity to a woman who gasped 'Great speech!' as they came? Possibly less than none. I'd just do lots and lots of jokes, largely because I rarely understood the arguments involved.

There was a real ethereal quality to the days of the big debates. I'd wake up really early with nerves and find my mum warming my good shirt by the fire and putting my shaving stuff out. It was a lot like doing comedy gigs later on. The nervousness dominated my whole day. On the bus trip to the school we'd be debating against, everyone else would be having a laugh but I'd be trapped in my fear bubble. Afterwards I'd be really excited, high and relieved, and there were often girls to talk to on the way back. I'd be back in my jokey mode, looking for the funny side of everything in the way that only an ingratiating virgin can. In hindsight, they must have all have thought that I was some kind of manic depressive.

We were one of the few comprehensives who'd do well in the debates, because we had such a good coach. After the first round or two you'd be up against a bunch of public schools. Scotland's public schools are pretty Lovecraftian: archaic and bizarre institutions dedicated to the production of humourless young adults. I'd never send my kids to public school, partly because I think it's socially divisive, but mainly because I think they generally produce shallow people. When my kids have their nervous breakdown in their twenties (everybody seems to have a nervous breakdown before thirty, but culturally we are trained not to mention this) I don't want the friends they have to fall back on to be a bunch of cunty, CV-padding, tax-discussing Scottish dentists and lawyers.

I used to quite enjoy standing underneath baroque paintings of former headmasters, debating in my stiff C&A shirts and NHS specs. I felt like Alf Tupper, Tough of the Track. We won a few gongs and got a glimpse into another world, a world of different nerds. Nerds who knew that their school bullies would one day work for them.

I suppose debating was my first real encounter with the class system. There was a guy from one public school we knocked out of a competition who refused to shake hands afterwards because we were comprehensive kids. The next time I saw him he was a left-wing student leader organising an anti-poll tax sit-in at Glasgow Uni. I sometimes wonder if anybody really has principles or if they're all just chasing different kinds of sex. Life isn't just a choice between Conservatives and Socialist Workers. It's also a choice between fucking a muscular polo player at an Oxbridge ball or being rattled in a caravan by your yoga teacher at a weekend of environmental awareness.

We are, of course, ruled by genetic inbreds. Most aristocrats have DNA so damaged they could join the X-Men. When I walk through Knightsbridge I feel like I'm on a mini-break in Chernobyl. You can tell what class you are by this simple test. There's a fox in your back garden. You're upper class if you get on a horse and chase it with a pack of hounds. You're middle class if you make your children draw a picture of it to send into *Blue Peter*. You're working class if you beat it to death with a shovel and make soup out of it. Upper-class people go to Oxford or Cambridge, middle-class people go to any other university. Working-class people go the university of hard knocks: Dundee Abertay. If my grandfather had died working down the Strathblane coffee mines, if Strathblane even had a coffee mine, he would be turning in his grave, rather than exposing himself to care workers in an Alzheimer's hospice, which I believe is what he's doing right about now.

The thing that really gets me about our upper classes is this: what's wrong with using an attic to store old lampshades and games of KerPlunk? What's this obsession with hiding inbred mutant children in the attic? That's the reason why you never see a member of the upper class in an episode of *Cash in the Attic*.

'This is a very unusual piece, do you know what it is?'

'Oh, that's Edward and Charles, the Siamese twins. I'd quite forgotten they were up here.'

There wasn't just a class divide in Glasgow – when I was growing up it was also pretty racist. Asian shopkeepers would get abuse and black footballers had bananas thrown at them. I don't know if the attitudes behind that have really gone away; maybe people are just better at hiding those feelings.

I used to think of Scotland as particularly racist but when I went to England I found it much the same. The other night a cabbie in London recognised me and asked if I ever got censored on the grounds of political correctness. I mumbled something about occasionally having things toned down and he said:

'I know. You can't call a coon a coon or a poof a poof, can you?'

It was amazing. This guy actually lives in a reality where everybody on *Mock the Week* is doing jokes about Obama's fiscal-stimulus policy and what we'd really rather be doing is saying, 'He is a coon.' Of course, neither country has anything on Ireland, which has a set of cheerfully racist attitudes worthy of the Third Reich. Then of course, there's Australia. It's ironic that Australians are so racist. Kind of hard to defend the proposition that black people don't belong in your country, when the white people keep dying from skin cancer.

When I watched the infamous *Celebrity Big Brother* that featured the bullying of Shilpa Shetty I started to consider that I might be one of the few people who isn't into racism and that I had totally underestimated its current level of coolness. One thing is certain, it doesn't do ratings any harm so we're going to try to build as much racism into the next series of *Mock the Week* as possible. Naturally, Hugh Dennis has raised objections but that is just the behaviour of a typical Chinky. Racism really does open up new markets to the canny performer. Jade Goody went from being an unknown in India to effigies of her being waved in the streets.

I've always been pretty broadminded about other cultures. For instance, I'm in favour of the full-length burqa as it allows me to masturbate in Tescos. The spectacle of British politicians playing to the assumption that we are all racists sickens me. I've come up with my own British Citizenship Test exam paper that would help make sure the applicant will fit in with the culture.

1. Spot the difference between these two cartoons of Mohammed.
2. Why has your country never voted for us in Eurovision?
3. Have you ever looked at the Ingredients on *Ready, Steady, Cook* and thought 'I could make a bomb out of that'?
4. You've just picked up a newspaper on your way to the Tube. Expecting to be shot?
5. Write down ten well-known British swearwords. On the house of your local paedophile.
6. A TV presenter has been involved in a sex offence. Do you find this (a) horrifying, or (b) a bit of a laugh?
7. Your mother has just died. How long do you spend talking to the doctor about football?
8. If you fail this British Citizenship Test, will you accept a taxi driver's licence?

Earlier this year Carol Thatcher was booted off *The One Show* for comparing a black tennis player to a golliwog. To be fair she does live in Knightsbridge, so the last time she saw anyone black was probably on a jar of Robertson's jam in the Seventies. When she saw Obama's inauguration speech she just thought it was just a long advert for marmalade. Her mother was just as confused. During the Brixton riots Margaret Thatcher thought she was watching the director's cut of *Noddy*.

Carol Thatcher obviously lives in a twilight world where everyone is a cartoon figure. She probably thought *The One Show* was being presented by Shrek. Actually for months so did I. Carol comes from a different generation; no doubt as a kid she had a golliwog – who shined the family silver, tended to the horses and gave her mum a right good seeing to once a month when Denis had gone to work.

Actually, the Queen recently came under fire for selling golliwogs. A palace spokesman said, 'We apologise unreservedly. They're a historical anomaly from another time. But they are the royal family and they'll do what they like.' The palace has now banned golliwogs from its royal shop in Sandringham. When Prince Philip heard this he said, 'Quite right too, and it's time to add public transport and restaurants to the list.' Is it the dolls that are offensive or the name? Perhaps they just need to be rebranded. I suggest a name change to 'Urban Barbie'. Carol believed she was sacked from the BBC because of a longstanding vendetta against her mother. Ridiculous. If the BBC really had a serious grudge against Margaret Thatcher surely they would have invested billions of the licence fee into developing an injectable dose of Alzheimer's disease that fellow guest David

Frost could have secretly administered to her when she appeared on a 1987 episode of *Question Time*. Oops, have I said too much?

The school had a nice policy of trying to do stuff for elderly people in the community. Every Christmas we'd be put into groups to make up a food parcel for the old fuckers. The teachers supervised but really only checked them by weight, so we'd try to make them as bizarre and unhelpful as possible. One year myself and the Marinelli twins gave someone a box containing two out-of-date industrial tins of pilchards from their dad's shop; every available flavour of Angel Delight; a tin of curried beans that had been in my house for so long it was almost an heirloom; and an almost complete pack of Top Trumps: Rally Cars.

A lot of us have felt ambivalent about old people at some point. Grandparents have a lot of annoying habits. Like dying just as you get addicted to their heart pills. Or owning a nice house and then not dying. If it wasn't for MRSA I'd never have managed to get my new kitchen. On the upside, the elderly do get their own seats on the bus. Albeit ones that stink of piss. But it does always amaze me how many seats on the bus are reserved for the elderly and infirm. Ever got on a bus and thought, 'Where's this thing going? Lourdes?'

In fifth year, my friend Craig and I volunteered for doing community work with the elderly one afternoon a week because it got us out of PE. We had two oldies we visited regularly. One was an old man called Mr Bowman. He was a really sweet old guy and we enjoyed his endless stories about Scottish history, something he had quite a poor grasp of. The weekly lecture was generally cribbed from a week-by-week periodical he got delivered called *Scotland's Story*. He would throw people from one era into another and add macabre details nobody could have known like he was a postmodern novelist.

There was an old woman too, whose name escapes me. We found her annoying because she actually wanted us to get her shopping and would send us to Woolworth's to get stuff for her, rather than make us tea and biscuits and improvise long lies set in the Jacobean period. If she was still alive now she'd have been dismayed at Woolies' demise. Although it is gone, the administrators are selling the name, so they say, 'Woolworth's will be back, but no one knows when or in what form.' That's quite frightening. Like you will be sitting watching *Loose Women* one day, and some red and white foam will start to seep under your door, and before you know it there is a 20-foot pick-and-mix aisle trying to kill your kids. Woolworth's has incurred the highest job losses in the recession so far, with 27,000 workers losing their jobs. Where WERE all these people? Usually Woolies was devoid of all human life except an 18-yard queue of old ladies trying to buy metal teapots from the one 17-year-old Saturday assistant. Where were these hordes of staff? 13 people in a back room individually unwrapping a hundredweight of cola cubes?

That old biddy had a huge hearing aid that whistled when it wasn't tuned in properly. We both learned to whistle without moving our lips and tilt our heads as if we could hear something. This would send her scurrying off to retune it and we could watch TV for ten minutes. She got wise to that trick, so to convince her it was on the blink Craig learned to talk in such a way that he just mouthed silently and said every third word.

The worst thing for Craig and me was that these oldies were getting more action than us. Apparently one in five Scots over 45 has sex without condoms. Who can blame them? If you still manage to get a stiffy at that age you don't want to hide it. You want to stick a sparkler in it and hold a news conference. Most men that age are married with kids anyway. Sex is like being a member of the National Trust. You get free entry to an old ruin, but you never use it. But I read a tragic story the other day. A 73-year-old man had his sight restored after more than 30 years with a bionic eye. Just in time to see the rest of his body packing up. All this time all he's had is the image of his beautiful young wife in his head. When he sees what she looks like now he's going to be in need of a bionic cock.

My school was a Catholic school so there was a fair bit of religious education. This somehow consisted almost entirely of pretty intense diatribes against abortion, with almost no reference to religion whatsoever. There was a school priest and once a month he came round to do questions and answers with the classes. It was a relief from the videos of foetuses but nobody could think of anything to ask him. We had guessed that he wouldn't have a clue about any of the stuff we wanted to know, because he was a priest.

'Where sells vodka if you're underage, Father? Do you know any slack lassies?'

It had become embarrassing that he just sat there being regarded silently and without curiosity, so one week our teacher tried to prime us before he arrived.

'You might want to ask Father why do priests wear dog collars?' he suggested. 'Or why is it that the Bible outlaws pork and yet we eat bacon?'

There was a long awkward silence as Father Hannaway took his seat. Craig, in his booming Irish voice, asked him,

'WHY DO PRIESTS WEAR SHOES?' Father Hannaway looked visibly shaken but seemed to be getting his head around it just as Craig followed up with,

'DO YOU EAT BACON!?'

He did that thing comics do, going for a tried-and-tested piece of material to steady himself. Anyone who had a genuine question had to make do with a lengthy explanation of what myrrh was.

Craig was constantly taking the piss and misanthropically causing trouble. He had a game he'd play where he'd clip little kids in the face with his bag. He had a real knack for it and could often knock them right onto their backs. I was always pestering him to show me the secret of his technique. One day he silently unzipped the side of his bag to reveal that it held a gigantic spanner.

I've always tended to have one enormously tall friend throughout my life, perhaps because I had one in my fantasy life as a kid. He was Irish and had loads of brothers and a sister. I hung out at their place a lot as a teenager. No doubt that was an enormous pain in the arse for everybody but as a kid you never notice those things. I thought of them as this really normal family, in contrast to living in my own quiet, undemonstrative house. Of course, once I'd witnessed a few displays of naked emotion, I began to appreciate the tranquil autism on offer at home.

We both started drinking when we were at school. There was a place all the kids would go where they served you underage. It was called the Outhouse and for a month or so one summer when I was about sixteen we'd all go down there and get pissed on vodka and orange and bottles of Grolsch. I used to really open up on a few drinks and would spraff on about whatever I was reading, generally to some bam from school who'd respond with chat about Celtic's lack of options on the bench. That pub got shut down for a wee bit and the rumour was that someone had gone in there to settle a grudge with an axe. The victim had bolted for the door and got it thrown between his shoulder blades. A really tricky skill that, you'd imagine. I hope that whatever song was on the jukebox had a bit of a drum roll just before he did it. It sounded fantastical, maybe it never happened and was just some teenage urban myth, but you were always running into people who claimed to have been there. Their stories matched closely enough that even as teenagers desperate for a drink and to stand in the same general space as some lassies, we never went back.

Everyone looked forward to house parties. That was where you could use the magic of alcohol to batter down sixteen years of Catholic repression and try to pump your chemistry partner. The best ones were where someone had an 'empty'. This meant that the parents were away and their children had decided, for the sake of popularity, to let a whole bunch of semi-acquaintances vomit on the carpets. These parties were very much like the War, people coming back from the same battle with different accounts of what had gone on – claims to have fingered, fought or dry-ridden people in various rooms and cupboards. There was a grotesque, crowing sexual boasting allowed from the victors. I remember one guy shouting into his friend's face at school,

'It was great to think of you trying to get to sleep on the living-room floor while I was next door getting sucked and fucked and allsorts!'

It was harder for kids to buy drink then, I think. There was often not enough booze at a party to stay drunk. I remember Craig and me standing on our heads against a wall and drinking cans of Bud through a straw in the hope of making it hit us harder. Sometimes the parents would leave slabs of pishy low-alcohol lager. We'd plough through ten cans each, wondering if making our bladders explode might give us a buzz.

I never really had any drive to be popular at school. There weren't really any groups that particularly appealed to me. I suppose the one group that I'd liked to have got in with was the Sluts. They already seemed to have plenty to occupy them though. It's not like girls at school weren't having sex; they just weren't having it with us. There were older boys with cars and money building a mighty sex dam way upstream. Our kind lived in parched lands fed by a trickle of ugly nymphos and nerdy girls who lost it on booze. I never got anywhere sexually at school. Neither did Craig. We both kind of despaired. I could feel how uncomfortably polite and attentive we were becoming to women. Every girl we met got treated like a much-loved, but now terminally ill member of a visiting royal family. They must have thought we were weird as fuck.

Lust is a big part of most men's personality. They just tend to make a point of denying it, so they can get more sex. In the summertime that noise you can hear isn't grasshoppers. It's the sound of men's teeth grinding as their rusty libidos crank up through the gears. I remember as a young man being told that men's sex drives tailed off after 17. That's just something they tell you to try to soften the blow. They can't tell you that you're looking at up to seventy years of feeling like a fox trapped on the other side of a chicken coop and an internet bill like a medium-sized export business.

Kingsley Amis (a married philanderer) described his sex drive as 'Like spending fifty years handcuffed to a lunatic'. I have found mine to be like living inside a burning building. No doubt about it, sunshine makes it all a lot more difficult. No wonder Middle Eastern countries get their women to cover up. There was probably a point in history when Iraq was a beautiful orchard before they shagged it into the dust.

Men are obsessed with breasts. I can still remember the first one I saw when, aged 11, an assistant bent over in Woolworth's. If there had been more of that sort of thing they might still be open. I have forgotten countless things since then (most of my childhood and all of Higher Physics), yet that breast is still burnt onto my retina like I've just been staring at a tit-shaped lightbulb. It's a peculiarity of men that we forget things like anniversaries and birthdays yet remember every flash of leg and glimpse of underwear. Perhaps as we get really old those are the only memories that will be left to us. Probably why we spend the last five years of our lives drooling. If I'd spent the time that I've spent thinking about sex on thinking about physics I could be world famous by now. For punching my way out of a bank vault with my robot tentacles.

There was a standard thing that happened at school where some dweeby kid would get surrounded and asked specific questions about sexual stuff. This would usually end in them making some tremendous faux pas – a girl called Elaine Doran once got pressured into saying that people got pregnant by pressing their bums together – and everyone would crow derisive laughter into their dejected face. On the more advanced stuff, I didn't have a clue either and just had to act confident and pretend I knew what was going on. A skill that came in useful when I started to have sex for real.

I first came when I was nearly 12. I'd been watching a movie called *Another Time, Another Place*, which starred Phyllis Logan in what looked like an unpromising tale of wartime island life in Scotland. She gets fucked twice. I was lying in shock in bed afterwards when my dick exploded. This was the night before we went on our summer holiday to Ireland. I spent six weeks locked in the bathroom wanking until my cock was a tattered pink flag of surrender. I tried to hide my burgeoning sexuality from my

MY GODPARENTS WITH WEE ME.

MY COUSINS IN IRELAND,
I'M ON THE FAR RIGHT.

MY SISTER JOINS ME AFTER MY EAR DEBACLE.

ARCHDUKE FRANZ FERDINAND AND HIS FAMOUS MECHANICAL BEEHIVE.

MY BROTHER,
SISTER AND ME
WITH THOMAS
DUFFY.

HOLY COMMUNION.

**ALWAYS GET A
HOLY COMMUNION
LANDSCAPE SHOT.**

THIS SORT OF THING HAPPENS
SO CASUALLY AT CHURCHES.

US.

IN IRELAND, TRYING TO CROUCH MY ENORMOUS HAIR INTO SHOT.

I THOROUGHLY RECOMMEND ECSTASY.

THE REVEREND AND CRAIG WOULD HOLD THESE POSES FOR HOURS BEFORE A SHOW.

LIVE FLOOR SHOW.

IN THE POLE-DANCING CLUB.

parents, but the fact they now spent half the household budget on toilet roll probably gave the game away.

There was a lady Hare Krishna who would hand out leaflets on my route back from school. I'd talk to her because she was quite attractive and I had this idea that maybe she would fuck me to get me to join; that maybe that was how it all worked. I actually got a book on Hare Krishna to see if Hare Krishnas were up for it. They are totally not. By this stage I couldn't pass her without speaking so I started to walk a much longer way home.

One of our English teachers was called Mrs Tait. She was about 30, a brunette, and wore tight sweaters, stockings and suspenders. It just about drove us all crazy. Thank God I wasn't in her class – it would have given me a nervous breakdown. For a while our English class was near hers. Her room faced onto the corridor and had frosted glass, except for a narrow strip near the ceiling. Craig and I would run down after Physics and jump up onto the window sill. We could see in, just, and watch Mrs Tait sitting on her desk with her legs crossed so you could see her suspenders. It was a class full of fifth years, the guys having that preoccupied, twitching look you normally only see in hostages. We weren't the only guys who'd jump onto the window – there was always somebody up there. Looking back, she must have been able to see our darting sets of eyes ten feet up the wall and probably our hard-ons pressed against the frosted glass. Years later I ran into one of my old teachers down the pub. 'I have a theory,' I told him, 'that Mrs Tait can't really have existed. She was a shared hallucination brought on by the hormones of hundreds of boys. She wasn't really like that but it's how we all agreed to see her. She was a construct.'

'I have a theory,' sighed my old teacher, draining his pint, 'that she was a fucking dirty cow.'

Of course I'd been programmed with a lot of Catholic guilt. Aged 12 I was mortified about the feelings I had for married women. I even showed some kind of morality. Whenever I wanked about my married English teacher, just before I came I'd think of one of the girls at school. Looking back, me ejaculating about a 15-year-old girl probably wasn't making God all that happy. When you're younger you don't realise that guilt is the engine of all that's truly arousing about sex. Adam and Eve probably had really boring sex before she ate that apple, gentle stuff surrounded by unnamed woodland creatures. Afterwards it would have been really intense shit with a snake wrapped around them. 'Who gives a shit about gardens anyway? There's a big rock just outside the garden we can fuck on! Tell God if he wants to make himself useful he can stick his finger up my arse!'

Recently, a Polish Catholic priest has published a book which provides married couples with a theological and practical guide to spicing up their sex lives. All 400 pieces of advice involve bringing a Catholic priest into your bedroom. Critics have questioned the competency of a celibate monk to write about sex. But then again, if you've been married more than two years then a celibate monk is probably getting more sex than you are.

In my early teens we had a black-and-white portable TV in our bedroom. I would tell my mum there was snooker on, then go to my room and try to watch any film I thought there might be sex in. The first time I saw full-frontal nudity was in the drama series *Tenko*. It was a female prisoner of war washing in a tin bath under armed guard but I felt no guilt. You got to see her fanny. When Channel 4 started their Red Triangle series of banned sex films my synapses melted. There'd be a couple of weeks of films with full-on sex scenes, then they'd throw in a film that had been banned because it featured the brutality of Turkish prison life. Still, the rewards were so great I'd even persevere with those ones. Somebody might get released from the prison and fuck someone! Or maybe a female lawyer would come in to work on somebody's case and they'd all fuck her! I was desperate. That red triangle on C4 served as a starting pistol for a wanking marathon. By the end I felt like I needed a foil blanket wrapped around me.

In those days if you glimpsed a nipple on TV it was like porn Christmas. Now any teenager with a laptop is just two clicks away from midgets fucking donkeys. I still have a good eye for when sex will appear on TV, a tragic talent really. A couple of years ago I was stuck in a hotel in London and noticed that there was a show on called *100 Funniest Movie Moments*. I gauged that Meg Ryan's fake orgasm scene from *When Harry Met Sally* would be in at around number 20 and I could crack one off to it. It was actually something like 21, so I had plenty of time to get back in the mood by the time they showed the rap scene from *Three Men and a Little Lady*. I'm glad they didn't keep going with that series: *Three Men and the Awkward Bathtime of a 16 Year Old* would have been horrible.

I'll never forget my first kiss, although granddad denies it. Actually, I was in a terrible nightspot called the Cotton Club and snogged my chemistry partner, locking onto her like a starving vampire. I had a cold, so for quite a while the air coming through her nose was the only oxygen getting into either of us.

Then, the summer after I left school was enlivened by suddenly, briefly getting a girlfriend. She was a student nurse living in the Red Road flats. For three weeks she'd let me come round and dry ride her on her living-room floor till 1 am, at which point she'd chuck me out into streets about as dangerous as wartime Berlin. After hours of near-sex I'd have probably made a reasonable attempt to fuck any assailant to death.

I sometimes have an out-of-body experience where I see myself deleting emails that promise me 'Live Sex Shows!' or 'Britney Spears Sucking Cock!' from the perspective of my 14-year-old self. The younger me can't believe how I take for granted the cornucopia of sexual possibility on offer, the blasé way in which I reject 'Nuns Fucking!' He had to make do with scraps of magazines found under hedges and strained glimpses of library assistants' knees.

Of course, with porn you could argue is it really these girls being exploited or is it in fact men's sexual responses that are being exploited? No, it's definitely these girls! I've always wondered, if surgeons can get porn actresses' tits to look so great, how come they can't do anything about that dead look in their eyes? How hard can it be to make contact lenses tinged with a bit of hope? I've seen sexier looks in the eyes of a snowman. I hate that look they have when they're picturing their father.

Apparently 66 per cent of women watch pornography, although that figure rises considerably if they've ever walked in on their partners when they think they are alone in the house. Jacqui Smith's husband was criticised for claiming expenses for watching two porn films. Why? He should be praised for his restraint. If I was married to a boiler like Jacqui Smith I'd have 24-hour porn pumped into my frontal lobe by fibre optics. I'd look like one of those monkeys you see on anti-vivisection posters. Look at it this way, it was either claim expenses on two dirty movies or go into Jacqui's bedroom and claim expenses on a fistful of Viagra, a bottle of vodka and a lifetime in psychotherapy.

Reports said she was 'livid and shocked' and has given her husband a 'real ear-bashing'. Maybe if she tried bashing another part of his body he might not watch so much porn. If you are really not up for it Jacqui then next time why not let him bash your ear. It can't get you pregnant! I wonder what the pornos were? Maybe Jacqui wouldn't have been so angry if they were political. May I suggest *Whorehouse of Commons, Black Rod and the Earlyday Motion* or the much-loved *A Member up the Dispatch Box*. When he made that public apology he looked incredibly embarrassed. So he should be. You can get all the porn you want online for free.

My porn habit is a bit like having malaria. It's not a huge problem but every few months I lose a couple of days to it. I'll sit down planning to look at it for half an hour and come to at four in the morning with the laptop having left a crop circle of electrical burns in my chest hair. I imagine that most men are the same and are just better or worse at hiding it. I think that in those old novels where men retire to one room to play billiards while the ladies go to the drawing room, the men are really working on old plans for the internet. Huge drawings of steam-powered computers get spread out as one guy clicks billiard balls together to maintain the charade. Nowadays there's Japanese porn, there's Russian porn but there are whole continents that haven't stepped up to the plate yet. Can you imagine what African porn is going to be like? There'll be bukkake movies that start like *Zulu* – a girl knowing that she's going to get fucked by the whole horizon. Or maybe their porn is just a 90-minute shot of a running tap.

Things are only going to get worse – BT is bringing in 40 MB broadband. They say it will herald a new dawn in communications and synergise media formats. Blah, blah, blah. The only reason anyone is getting excited is it means feature-length porn films in seconds, instead of sitting there with the Kleenex and *The Big Book of Sudoku*. Personally I think this universal access to limitless, high-definition porn will destroy civilisation more surely than a direct asteroid hit. There's a horrible irony in the fact that the machine we have to use for most of our work contains the most distracting imagery possible. Writing this book has taken a tremendous act of will. You know why *War and Peace* is so long? Tolstoy's inkwell didn't have tiny people fucking in it.

I have a theory that our sex drives were put in place to keep us talking to each other, so we make progress as a species. There were whole years where I'd never have left the house if I hadn't been trying to get laid. I'm vaguely in line with the Freudian thing that everything we do is an attempt to get more sex. Look at the space shuttle. Those scientists built that so they could tell ladies about it. Could it look more like a giant metal dick? I don't even think they need that main fuel tank – it's just an aesthetic cock flourish.

The male sex drive definitely feels like more of a curse than a blessing. I was in Berlin on my holidays this year and went to every museum, a standard middle-class non-drinker's way of pretending that he can enjoy himself. There's one that has the whole entranceway to a Babylonian temple. You can literally walk down a whole corridor that looks exactly as it would when you were coming through the ancient city of Babylon – it's beautiful. Before I walked down it I tried to empty my mind and imagine I was actually an ancient Babylonian, going to make a sacrifice. Every step of the walk I was transfixed by the visible top of a German tourist's knickers, and the washing instructions sticking out of them.

I think there is a lot that we don't understand about our sex drives. Scientists have discovered that apes will exchange meat for sex. And by scientists I mean a clinically depressed butcher going through a rather messy divorce. If a male chimpanzee shares meat with a female he will double the amount of times he can copulate with her. That probably explains why I've been taking bunches of bananas up to the zoo and getting nowhere! Forget apes, I'll exchange meat for sex. I've got everything we need to start the transaction: a freezer full of Turkey Twizzlers and a hard-on. And yes, that is my most recent Facebook update. I might not get to shag a monkey but there's a fighting chance Fern Britton will be in touch.

SIX

The summer I left school I got a job as a library assistant, my first opportunity to really bond with homosexual men and women going through the menopause. I was really unbelievably terrible at it, as I have been at every job I've had. The problem is this: all jobs seem to involve receiving a certain amount of oblique sniping or criticism that you are supposed to put up with. I simply can't be fucked, not even a little bit. On the first day in that job an old posh gent had a go at me for some forgotten reason and I told him to fuck off. I think he was so shocked that he literally couldn't process it and just wandered off.

When I was growing up the library had a truly shit selection. A biography section labelled 'Famous Lives' is always a bad sign. The library was just somewhere warm to go that was out of the house. As a consequence I read everything there that interested me and had to start on things that really didn't. I've read quite a few terrible thrillers by Hammond Innes and Frederick Forsyth. For some reason, men in Glasgow seem to really relate to the adventures of doomed commercial pilots roped into a mercenary gun-drop by old army buddies. On the off-chance that you are reading this and an old army buddy has recently proposed something like this to you, he has money/woman problems and is planning a double-cross.

There were loads of books of old Scottish memoirs that I'd never have read if there was anything else, and I absolutely loved them. Molly Weir, who played Hazel the McWitch in *Rentaghost*, wrote some really interesting books about her life. Of course by the last one she seems to have gone mad in show business and spends the first chapter talking about buying a really big house and having it re-carpeted. Cliff Hanley I liked too. Those books really brought it home that for all the dullness of my life, it lacked what until then had been the defining characteristic of life for every other generation in that city: poverty.

It was around this time that I really got into the work of Noam Chomsky. He's good at explaining where we are at and warning us about where we're going. I always remember a thing in one of his books where he says that capitalism can't have everything its own way because it will 'create a hell that no rational person would want to live in'. Noam has never been on ScotRail, so doesn't know that we are already there.

I got into Chomsky because I heard Bill Hicks talk about him in an interview. Bill Hicks is my favourite comedian and really was sort of a political thinker in his own way. It always amuses me to hear comedians say he's an influence on them, because you never see any evidence of it. The people who say that are always the sort of guys who would shit balloon animals through a burning hoop if it got them doing a reaction show to *I'm a Celebrity* on ITV 9.

Another writer I follow is George Monbiot. He writes about climate change, the general political landscape of Britain and, eh, growing fruit. I think all his stuff is on www.monbiot.com and I'd recommend it. I'd even recommend the stuff about recondite fruit-growing knowledge. His work will lead to either a highly politicised fruit-growing lobby or revolutionaries who are really, really fussy about apples.

There was a really attractive assistant working at our library. She wore very short skirts and was really bad tempered, something which I've always liked. She was the first person I really masturbated about. There was one straight, married guy who worked in that library and it looked like her presence wore him down considerably. He drifted around with a grim look in his eye, sweating like he had malaria. Once I had a huge argument with her about an overdue book. When I got home I found that, during the course of the argument, I had ejaculated.

There was a big comedy-record collection there that I took out and taped everything. It was amazing to find that comedy didn't have to be shit. Going from watching Jimmy Tarbuck doing old Irish gags on *Live from Her Majesty's* to hearing classic *Goon Shows* or Peter Cook and Dudley Moore or a Billy album was a real shock. I suppose we all have this naïve idea that the best stuff will find its way onto TV. That's pretty much the opposite of the truth.

That was the start of wanting to be a comedy writer. I used to sit and write, imagining that one day I could get one of those jobs where everybody sat in a room drinking coffee and writing lines. I read *Billy Liar* and the stuff where he wanted to be a joke writer didn't read like foolish daydreaming; it seemed a totally rational aspiration to me. We got taught that book at school and everybody took his desire to get out of his home town and do something creative as naïve idiocy. I thought that said quite a lot about Glasgow.

Most of the people I knew stayed on to do sixth form but Craig and I went to Langside College for a year. It's a place in Battlefield that I would heartily recommend if you want to meet nutters, lust after unobtainable Indian women and smoke hash. Any given class might have mothers who were doing a class as a hobby, vocational types doing it to get onto another course or mental cases who'd been made to do it to get their bursary. It was probably the only glimpse of anything approaching the real world I've ever had, and it was terrifying.

I got into the drama society and acted in a play. Dressed in shorts and a tank top, I played a 12-year-old boy and was several inches taller than the guy playing my dad. A lot of people who came said they thought that I was playing someone with a mental handicap. There were a couple of proper actors in it. I've always really appreciated acting as a talent. It's taken for granted but when you see somebody who's really good it's so compelling. I found the proper actors there to be quite a bitchy bunch. Mind you, if I saw stand-up comics having exactly the same conversations they'd sound so positive I'd assume they were being sarcastic.

This was when I first started to put on weight. I've had to really battle with my weight ever since; it's a real slog. In those days obesity wasn't really an issue in the way it is now. I don't think we really related the fact that we were all getting fatter because of all the beer we drank. Ever since college I've had to work at never really being slim but never quite reaching properly fat. I swim just enough for my weight to hover somewhere between compliments and abuse. Apparently scientists recommend 3,000 steps in half an hour for moderate exercise. Not only a good way to get fit but also a perfect way to develop obsessive compulsive disorder. One, two, three, feeling fit, one thousand and four … must keep going … two thousand and seventy nine … going absolutely mental. Light switch on. Light switch off.

They say fat people make better lovers. Who says this? Fat virgins. But of course, the debate about size zero models continues. Isn't it about time that we insisted that all modelling campaigns should be done by models with normal measurements? And then pretend to find them attractive. I'm joking. There's a fallacy that men are attracted by advertising images of very thin women in underwear. Actually, we're attracted by most women in their underwear. In fact, just show us the underwear lying over the back of a chair. We'll buy your toothpaste.

At Langside I started hanging around with a guy called Joe who was about 22 and a complete basket-case. He'd been a full-on soccer casual and was a very bad guy. He ran a combat club somewhere in the East End. I went along to watch them one time. Always a bad sign to see everybody unpacking weapons in the changing room. The training seemed to involve them leaping from wall-bars onto the ground in a bid to strengthen their legs, followed by punching each other in the stomach while shouting. They had something that most properly trained fighters lack. Madness.

Joe was a dangerous nut but had a bright, plausible manner that generally got everybody onside. I remember once seeing him trying to get his girlfriend out of her physics class; he wandered right through the door with her arguing. When the teacher turned up and asked him what he was doing there he said he was going class to class raising money for the family of a murdered schoolgirl. The teacher gave him a fiver.

Along with another guy, we promoted a club night. We hired a nightclub in the town and sold tickets on campus and even made some money. Joe said we should use the profits to buy a gun, so that 'nobody will fuck with us'. I spent my half on a Walkman.

One night we were coming home from town and some wee guys started shouting at us from halfway down Buchanan Street.

'Take this,' growled Joe, handing me a lump of metal on a length of cord. He pulled a bottle out of his jacket and charged downhill, unaware that I was legging it the other way.

Eventually, I found a taxi but as I was getting in Joe caught up with me and jumped in too. He was furious that he'd had to 'run from anybody in the toon!' I viewed getting away from a fight to be quite a result, but obviously couldn't say that as the madman frothed on. When we got out of the cab, he broke his bottle on a fence and held it to my throat. He was screaming and certainly seemed to be building up to stabbing me with it when some couple came by and asked what was going on. Thank fuck for pretty much the only people I've ever known to get involved when they see something like that.

That night in bed, I tried to think of how I could escape this maniac. We had a couple of club nights lined up and I was terrified. I thought about telling him that I had a bad heart, a congenital defect that meant I could die if exposed to the least excitement and thus, regrettably, I would have to terminate out friendship. Fuck, I was desperate.

What I did was to tell him that I was emigrating to Ireland, where I had a job. I only had a couple of classes a week, so I sneaked into them wearing a hat and left by the fire escape. Extreme, but it worked. I never saw him again but Joe will definitely have killed somebody by now.

The amusing thing was that my parents really warmed to the guy. He'd been to the house a couple of times and they thought he'd be a good influence. Old people are terrible judges of character. That's why daytime TV is full of people like David Dickinson who have criminal records. 'Oooh, he's a lovely man.' No, he's a convicted fraudster. There's always some presenter on those shows who turns out to have been a burglar. In many ways, I think old people's lack of character judgement is part of a sublimated desire for death. They suppress the part of themselves that warns them not to allow this stranger into their home, secretly hoping to be defrauded of the money they need to survive or to be bludgeoned to death with their own umbrella stand.

The summer I finished college I applied for a job working in the civil service. I only wanted something for the summer but had to pretend in the interview that I wanted to spend my life there, sorting forms, phoning people, filing things. I lied so much in the interview that it sounded like heavy sarcasm and got the job. It was truly terrible. I don't know how anybody can work in an office. The tense, political subtext to everything that happens is hellish.

I had a magnificently bleak job. There was a big book of everybody in Customs and Excise who was off sick. I'd have to keep the book up to date by phoning them at home for details of their illnesses. Loads of people were just off with 'stress'. That's our word for it, but it might just as well be 'horror'. There was a guy who had gone missing and I had to phone his distraught wife at intervals and check that he hadn't turned up. While he was missing he was still on full pay, but if he turned up some irregularity meant it would get cut to half.

Once, I phoned a guy at Fort William because his doctor's line was completely illegible. Fort William is under a military flight path and just as he was telling me what was wrong with him he was drowned out by jets. I asked him again and more jets drowned him out. The third time, just as the jets stopped, he really shouted it: 'I had genital herpes!' That was followed by the tense silence of someone who has just announced that he has genital herpes to his entire office. He knew he'd fucked his chances at the Christmas party and hung up without another word.

I suppose the only real advantage of a job is the licence to steal. The stationery from that job got me through university, where people would be baffled to see me taking notes in a leather-bound accounting ledger. Toilet rolls are the main item stolen by office staff. It used to be Post-it notes but people found they weren't as absorbent. The whole thing was only discovered because people kept stealing Post-it notes and sticking up messages reminding themselves to steal toilet rolls.

There was obviously the problem of me just not being able to do a job, at all. I'd get really bored and just go out for a pint. Or sit on the fire-escape smoking. My 'boss' was a 22-year-old guy who wore a vest under his shirt, and the idea of having to do what this guy said just seemed ridiculous. Even more than at school, everybody seemed eager for their lives to be mapped out for them. Most of the people in my job were 19 or 20 and they were all married or engaged, all talking about where they wanted to be in the civil service in twenty years' time. They seemed like rats guzzling down some sugary poison in a lab experiment.

One night I went to the pub with them all on Friday after work. I found the chat really terrifying; the two guys who worked the same desk as me were both trying to get on the office golf team to impress the boss. It was like something you'd heard about people doing in the 1950s. In Japan. We were celebrating a guy in the office getting engaged, at 19, to somebody on another floor of the building. A stripper came in, complete with blank eyes, Caesarean scar and wedding ring. I'm sure I could have one day fitted in with those guys. By sustaining quite a serious brain injury. Eventually, I think I just stopped going in and got sacked.

This was the time of the Poll Tax being introduced a year early in Scotland, to see how it went down. It went down really, really badly and they kept going with it regardless. I went on marches and sit-ins and the like. It was great to see people organising and protesting against something so unjust and brutal. Of course, those people took a lot of flak in the press, as if stopping bailiffs from emptying poor people's houses could ever make you the bad guys. I never paid the Poll Tax and got a bill for my arrears years later when I was at uni. I wrote 'Singapore?' on the envelope, burnt a hole through it with a fag and sent it back. I never heard from them again.

For all I hated Thatcher, Labour has been much, much worse. Perhaps a side effect of coming into political power is to develop a hatred of ordinary people. Nobody has ever really explained the urge to impose pointless, unworkable policies that dehumanise folk. Take ID cards, for example. There are a lot of practicalities about the ID-card scheme that the government doesn't seem to have taken onboard. Like how are they going to get fingerprints off people from Irvine? It's going to take at least a couple of hundred thousand years for their hoofs to evolve that far. And how do you actually prove who you are when you sign up for an ID card? Show them your passport? Well if that's proofs of identity, how about we use that instead of a fucking identity card?

Our political culture is now so debased that we regularly hear 'do gooders' getting the blame for things. Enviromentalists trying to stop a coal-burning power plant or a new runway that will (let's just remember) DESTROY THE EARTH are branded as our enemies, these 'do gooders'. Like doing good is a bad thing. You read all the time in the press that 'do gooders' are to blame – a sweepingly derogatory term. Or even worse, the 'so-called do gooders'. I've never once read that the blame was being put fairly and squarely on 'cunts', and let's face it 'cunts' must be behind fucking things up far more things than 'do gooders'. If it's not 'cunts' then I blame those 'so-called cunts'.

There's a lot of scapegoating around environmental issues. People criticise Ryanair and other low-budget airlines for encouraging people to fly. Come on, we all know that anyone flying by Ryanair will be doing at least half the journey by shuttle bus. But it's the animals I feel sorry for. In the animal versus human wars we've pretty much won about as complete a victory as it's possible to win. I mean, we still need to keep a close eye on the ants rising up, but as far as everything else goes we've pretty much stamped our dominance on their hairy faces, repeatedly – the ones we haven't wiped out completely probably long for extinction as a release from us eating them and parading around in front of them wearing the skins of their relatives.

Once, my friend Scott and I took his kids to a safari park. A brutal experience where both man and beast are equally demeaned. It started off – as all safari parks do – with a ride through the monkey enclosure. There were no monkeys. The rumour was that they had proved themselves too mischievous with the cars. They'd overstepped the line between cute-pulling-at-the-windscreen-wipers mischievous and the-safari-park-management-are-having-us-all-killed mischievous. So you spent the first ten minutes driving through an empty piece of scrubland where some monkeys used to live.

There's a thing called Chimp Island there. What would you put on Chimp Island? I'm sure that if you and I each sat down to design ourselves a Chimp Island, they'd both end up being very different. On the other hand, I think we'd both plant some fucking trees. The chimps just sat there on this little island with that grim look you see on the faces of lifers in prison documentaries. Their faces said, 'One day the wind will blow that boat over here and there will be a Great Reckoning.'

There were attractions where you could get much closer to the animals. There was a Vietnamese pot-bellied pig. Somebody had taken advantage of his friendliness to ram a HB pencil deep into his back. It had never been removed and some skin had grown around it. There was a cute little otter cheeping away in his enclosure. 'Look,' I offered to the kids, quite relieved at seeing something that didn't immediately fill me with horror, 'the little chap is saying "Hello!"'

One of the keepers sidled up to us. 'Naw, he's not saying "Hello!" His mate died last week … that's him crying.'

Scotland is always releasing stuff back into the wild, seriously overestimating itself as a place that an animal would choose to live. The zoos are just as bad. Why do they think that pandas are going to have any more success breeding at Edinburgh Zoo? Not even people like having sex out of doors in Scotland. I can't see the point, unless they're planning on taking the pandas to T in the Park. The pandas had to go to Edinburgh and not

Glasgow. A female with two black eyes in Glasgow? You'd have had local guys breaking into the compound and declaring their love. More and more people are going to zoos in this country, not because they're interested in the animals but because they want to see what life could be like with three guaranteed meals a day and a roof over your head. It's notoriously difficult to get pandas to mate, and some zoos even resort to showing them videos of 'panda porn'. Well, that's not going to help conception, that's just going to increase his late-night trips to get 'more bamboo' while he sneaks into the warden's office to rifle through DVDs of David Attenborough.

They're doing all sorts of weird stuff with genetics these days. They're unravelling the DNA code, cutting it up and splicing it together, implanting it and interbreeding species. They're putting pigs' hearts into humans instead of meat pies. They're putting DNA from beavers into elephants and now huge rogue beavers are going on the rampage and elephants are building dams before they go off to find the beavers' graveyard.

Researchers have also developed a genetically modified monkey. The monkeys were injected with a gene from a jellyfish that makes them glow in the dark and will one day help those that are seriously ill. What do they mean 'one day'? They could help now. If I was seriously ill and I was given a glow-in-the-dark monkey, I'd start feeling better pretty much instantly. If they could invent a kitten that shits candy floss that would cheer me up even more.

Shortly after being sacked from the civil service, I found out that the university place I had doing American Literature fell through because the course got axed. I managed to get on a similar course at Sussex University but I had to wait a year to start. I desperately wanted to get away from home so I took a place on clearing at Aston University, just so that for that year I could have a grant and get out of the house.

The course I went on was inexplicably terrible. 'Urban Planning and Policy' or something like that. I just did absolutely nothing. I know people say they did nothing on a course and really they mean they didn't work hard enough to do them-selves justice. I literally did nothing. It was such a grisly subject, filled with people who'd got it as a booby prize in clearing, but they never threw you out. The dissertation at the end of one term was on the subject 'Shopping Trends In Birmingham 1974'. My dissertation was handwritten, two pages long and entitled 'Shopping Trends in Birmingham 1974: Who Honestly Cares?'

Aston University was, and I'll wager still is, full of cunts. Most of the courses were engineering and technical stuff, and the largest society on campus was the Conservative Club. I lived in halls in Handsworth. It was like a practical joke – dropping a whole bunch of horrible Tory fuckers into the scene of a recent race riot. The result was that everybody holed up in halls, ate all their meals there and drank at the union bar. It was like a colonial hotel in a Graham Greene novel.

I had to share a room with a bloke called Andy, an engineer, keen hockey player and a worthless human being. Andy was a dull, sporty nonentity who never really penetrated anybody's consciousness; people who had met him several times had no idea who he was. It was like living with a ghost. He hated sharing a room and was always tense and grumpy. He had some posh sporty mates and they were always playing boorish pranks on people. One night when I was coming home pissed, Andy and his mates threw me into a bath of cold water. It was the sort of thing you were supposed to give and take there. I hated him for it in the deep, vengeful way a hero hates in a Spaghetti Western.

Luckily his engineering course seemed to involve a full day of lectures, while I had barely any and often just didn't go. His chief evening activity was to write long, tortuous letters to his girlfriend at home asking why she wouldn't have sex with him. I would read these when he was out, marvelling at the incredible weirdness of this seemingly ordinary man. One letter contained the amazing sentence, 'Maybe love is just a stronger kind of like, i.e. Love = Like + 2.' I didn't really smoke but when I learned of Andy's dislike of smoking and intense paranoia about cancer I always made sure to have a few ciggies in there every day. He spent the whole first term brewing barrels of homebrew wine beside his bed and when he was away at the weekends I would piss in them.

I lived quite a drunken, dissolute life there for a bit. One Sunday I was going out to get a newspaper with a crippling hangover when a minibus pulled up. It was this guy from my course called Paul and the entire Irish Society Gaelic football team. They had a game but were a man short so I was dragged into the back of this van and awarded the position of goalie. I couldn't wear my specs so I just stood there in my Hush Puppies and some borrowed shorts, dreading the first attack. I caught the ball cleanly and stood there feeling quite chuffed. In Gaelic football the strikers are allowed to charge the keeper into the net, and they did. We took a horrendous beating, then drank for two days.

It actually took me quite a while to get used to the range of English accents. I know everybody slags off Dick Van Dyke for his terrible Cockney accent in *Mary Poppins*. Nobody mentions the fact that if he'd got the Cockney accent spot on he'd have sounded like an even bigger cunt. England has, of course, done a lot of terrible stuff in its history. Scotland didn't do any of that. We just helped them. If the story of the world were a movie, Scotland would be an evil henchman.

I was still very much interested in comics, and my mates and I did a little comic strip for the student newspaper called 'Mute Dad'. It featured a dad who would just hit his son with all the standard parental clichés, but had to mime them because he was a mute. Nobody who read it had a fucking clue what it was about.

I had to pass an interview at Sussex to be sure of my place. I went down there on the National Express coach, a manned Portaloo of unbelievable depravity that I'd have to get used to over the next few years. As we pulled into Brighton I saw a beautiful girl sitting at the side of the road wearing a cardboard sign saying, 'I may be Janet Ellis', and thought the town would probably be good for a bit of a laugh. Instead of what I'd think nowadays, 'You pointless student bastard.' I missed my coach home and hung about on the pier till it closed, then slept in the entrance alcove at the side of the cathedral. Once I heard I'd got my place at Sussex I bailed from Aston, feeling that I had wrung what mirth I could out of it.

It was hard going back home, even for the six months before my course began, because without a grant I had no money and just fuck all to do. I knew that I was completely unable to hold down any kind of job, and Pollokshaws was like a tribute to boredom. If I were a budgie I'd have started pecking my own feathers out. I think boredom is a much-ignored factor in mental problems. In *Groundhog Day*, Bill Murray would probably have raped and killed Andie MacDowell quite a few times, really gone to town. I can see why they left that bit out of the movie. Bill Murray character's real triumph is that he can still eventually fall in love with someone after he has spunked on her disembodied colon.

I had a friend nearby from primary school. He was called Charlie Baker (the guy from the school drawing competition, remember him?) and over the years he had blossomed into a fully fledged eccentric. He wore three-piece tweed suits, or sometimes tight shorts and a straw boater. We'd go and get drunk together and talk pretentious shit. He was a good human being and it was inspiring to know somebody round there who was further off the map than me.

Charlie wrote short stories and little plays of a gruesome, violent and deliberately alienating nature. He would then submit these to various dull writing competitions, just to appal everybody. He was obsessed with certain things and they'd often turn up in the stories. He was obsessed with Robert Nairac, the SAS spy murdered by the IRA in the 1970s, the actress Greta Scacchi and James Bond. Versions of these, and often all three, would turn up in the violent, sexualised submissions he'd make to things like Strathclyde Library's 'Stories of Scotland' competition. They'd be expecting reminiscences of wartime Glasgow, not a sexually deviant spy abducting a major actress at gunpoint.

There was an air of Joe Orton about his dedication to horrifying nobody in particular. He wrote a brilliant story for a competition to celebrate England hosting the European Football Championship. It was called 'Playing for England' and involved a description of two England players putting in a series of horrendous challenges during a match. They both get sent off, but it all turns out to be a ploy they've concocted so they can fuck each other in the dressing room.

I started to think of myself as depressed, partly because I thought it would be quite cool to be depressed. I think really I was just a bit bored and disgusted with my surroundings. My

GP referred me to a weekly group-therapy session, I think to give me a taste of what genuinely depressed people looked like. It was actually sort of hilarious. The first session involved us all sharing our likes and dislikes. A wee guy who'd been completely silent piped up with a comprehensive list of his personal hatreds, reeling off the names of several professions, character types and family members. It was the most fluent display of casual disgust that I have ever heard. A couple of people in the room got namechecked and there was a long pause before he finished by spitting out with inexplicable venom, '... and fucking postmen!'

Genuinely depressed people seemed a lot more troubled than me; it really gave me some perspective on what I was. An angsty, adolescent dick. Some of the people there were really very amusing in a cynical, downbeat way. One guy was a cartoonist and showed me a comic strip he'd done about panic attacks. It was really good, autobiographical and done in the style of a sort of modern-day 'Oor Wullie'. There was a terrific bit in it of him having a panic attack trying to get off a train. There was something really funny and horrifying about seeing this wee Oor Wullie type clutching at his chest and thinking he was having a heart attack.

I had to do a speech about something one week. I worked hard on it and tried to make it really funny. Tough crowd, the depressed. Not a titter. As I walked back to my seat, the wee guy who had given the speech about likes and dislikes looked at me and said in an unbelievably mournful voice, 'That was funny.' He spoke in that voice constantly, so I'll never know if he was being sarcastic. I eventually left after about a month when it was announced that we had to go on a fieldtrip to see Scottish rockers Runrig. I'd decided that I wasn't actually depressed but Runrig might well tip me over the edge.

It was round about this time that I really got to know Paul Marsh, with whom I'd been on the debating society at school. I remembered writing a piece for one of his speeches and being absolutely amazed that he did it. It was all about how perhaps our reality is simply a zoo for aliens and they each have one of us that they watch as a pet. While some aliens will have Harrison Ford and find it delightfully entertaining, others will have to observe some junkie sleeping all day and occasionally retching into a stolen handbag. In the context of a second-year debate it might as well have been a high-pitched Russian naval ballad with maths for lyrics.

That's Paul   he's inexplicable. If I had to honestly try, I'd say he's like a flavour you've been hypnotised to forget or a long-lost Scottish Christmas movie from the 1970s that contained blasphemous scenes nobody remembered shooting after being filmed on a site of occult significance.

Now a more skilful writer would build a character up gradually; perhaps some anecdotes about their early life would give the reader an insight into the man they become. I'm just going to hit you with it. Give you an example and see if you can grasp Paul Marsh. OK. One time, Paul had to charge a magical sigil he'd made to create world peace. To do this he recorded a tropical calypso single that he released on the internet called 'Peace Mango'. Bam. Paul Marsh.

He wasn't always quite the way he is now, but the seeds were there. He was a bit of a reactionary when I first knew him, pretty much a Tory. I remember giving him the first *Invisibles* comic. If you've not read it, you definitely should. It's a crazy countercultural primer by Grant Morrison that we were into for years. I can still see that first issue flying across his bedroom as I threw it to him. He got into a lot of esoteric stuff off the back of that and the world lost an electronics journalist and gained a psychonaut.

Actually, while we're on the subject of things you should read, get all of Grant Morrison's comics – just go on Amazon or whatever and do it now. Mark Millar and Alan Moore are things you should get into too; there's a density and care in their comics that I've struggled to find in modern fiction. My favourite fiction writers are James Ellroy, Thomas Pynchon and Gene Wolfe. I never meet anybody who reads Gene Wolfe, and it's sad. He's often labelled as sci-fi or fantasy, but really 'genre fiction' is just a construct to stop people from finding interesting things to read. There are vested interests who'd rather that you were reading about some prick's midlife crisis in Hampstead instead of something that might change your life, like *The Invisibles* changed Paul's.

Paul and I did quite a lot of drinking before I had to go off to Sussex. Paul's mum used to get him a big slab of beer every week. We'd go out clubbing and then head back to his and drink until we passed out, playing a fighting game he had for the Atari that was less than worthless.

For some reason, we fell in with a group of gays and would go to gay clubs quite a bit. We were nineteen and had the idea that gay clubs would be full of straight, fag-haggy women who would assume we were gay, giving us the element of surprise. The gay clubs, it turned out, were full of poofs.

There was a straight girl called Babs in our group who developed a stalkerish love for Paul. She was a pretty full-on Catholic and was always bringing him gifts and tokens of her affection. I remember sitting with him at the end of some party she'd shown up to. For some reason Babs had bought him a cappuccino maker and he was using the cup it came with as a makeshift ashtray. One time we all went to a club and Paul started getting off with a random woman who was clearly wasted. She passed out and Babs came out of the toilets to see Paul attempting to shake her back to consciousness. The last we heard she had gone to Lourdes and perhaps became some kind of nun.

One of Paul's key traits is the delivery of bizarre, esoteric, absurd or terrifying information as if it were a commonplace truism. I once met him off a plane for a week's holiday in Barcelona. Eschewing the usual pleasantries, his posited the theory that the sun may have a consciousness. He'd been terrified on the plane because he'd been given a pen that is supposedly used by astronauts and was worried it might explode at altitude. Even though it's designed to go into fucking space.

We took acid together one time and I tried to raise the psychic shields necessary for that drug. Acid is sort of like having your psyche shaken about in the mouth of a huge beast. The inventor of LSD died aged 102 this year. At least he died the way he wanted … riding a winged centaur into the belly of a giant worm. Just as we started to trip Paul told me of his recent readings that proved that the earth was about to be hit by an asteroid. That weighed on my mind slightly to be honest.

Paul has turned me onto a lot of great stuff. The best one is something he told me about at a Hogmanay party we were at in the nineties.

'You know David Icke?'

'Yeah.'

'Have you read his new book?'

'No. What's he saying?'

'Well, he seems to be saying that the royal family and lots of politicians and, eh, country singers and famous people are, eh, sort of Lovecraftian lizards from the lower-fourth dimension.'

Go Dave. Yes, former Coventry goalkeeper David Icke's books are a joy. They are at once a feat of imagination and a genuine attempt to understand reality. He believes that everybody in a position of power is a serial-killing, shape-shifting lizard. I'm kind of behind him on this in that I think they may as well be fucking lizards. In fact being a lizard would actually make their behaviour more explicable. My favourite bit is a drawing in one of the books of a huge lizard wearing a robe and wielding a dagger. The caption reads, 'An artist's impression of Ted Heath'.

The other reason I remember that party so well is because it was the last memory I had to draw on for quite a while. I woke up in a park two days later, covered in bruises and clutching a dessert spoon. Happy New Year.

EIGHT

Going to Sussex University was great. Yes, a lot of the people were daft, middle-class cunts, but they were often pretty attractive and a relief from the crushing conformity of Scotland. I enjoyed the first few weeks of being on campus, the attitude of optimism and hope that held together while everybody liked each other. The atmosphere that I helped to destroy.

I lived in halls with a group of unsatirisable Americans, some Goths and a good-looking drug dealer guy who took one look at us all and never really spoke to us again. We'd see him occasionally drift into his room with a different attractive hippy girl every so often, but he'd clearly realised everybody else was a desperate loser. People had friends over from other halls and we were a regular community for a bit, until we realised that we had nothing in common but incipient alcoholism, and all social interaction went down to grunts.

One regular visitor to our hall was a tedious Goth who believed herself to be a psychic. People who ask you if you've ever seen a ghost are always people who believe in ghosts. They're limbering up to tell their own ghost story. These are always remarkably tedious efforts about feeling as if someone had brushed past them but nobody being there. I always think that if you're lying anyway you should at least make it interesting. At the very least, say that when you play football, the ghost of an old player who died after being struck by lightning appears to run alongside you, offering advice.

Another good tactic to get out of these conversations is to evince complete disdain for anybody who would believe in ghosts, but display a passionate conviction in the existence of 'Space Wolves'. This works best if you have already primed other onlookers to join in with their own worrying experiences at the paws of the Space Wolves. Allow for a good half an hour of shared reminiscences of these intergalactic scavengers and their pitiless forest planet. It will then be particularly galling for the ghost-story teller to have everybody laugh uproariously at their memory of seeing their grandfather's face at a window.

My own feeling is that ghosts are probably the unquiet spirits of people who, during their lives, were sexual voyeurs. Why else would they keep hanging around? You felt a strange draught in the room? That's him pulling his zip down. Get a medium in.

'I'm getting something from the other side ... it's the man who used to live here ... he wants you to ... shit on a glass-topped coffee table.'

For a while I did a phone-in on a campus radio show called *The Voice of America*. It was presented by an enormous, bearded American called Brad who was utterly devoid of humour in the way that only an American can be. He was notorious on campus for his banality and mirthlessness, being showered with pint glasses at the karaoke every week where he always sang a perfect rendition of 'Rawhide'. People listened to his show to hear the compellingly unironic way he'd introduce the Eagles or Chicago, and I'd man the phone lines to repel the constant complaints with extreme abuse. It was my stated intention to get Brad's show banned. He could never work out if I was joking and, looking back, there's a good chance he might have been a psychopath. I remember this as being some of the funniest work I've done, but clearly I was drunk. I'm sure every raving tramp in the street thinks he's delivering a satirical monologue.

Clearly, our campus, like any campus, was full of cunts. There was a group of really lame Italian exchange students who'd go around halls with an acoustic guitar, crashing parties and singing terrible rock ballads. The whole place was full of the sort of pussies that make me think that cockroaches might take over the earth without a nuclear war. There were some of the dullest people in the world there and they all seemed to have brutally dismissive nicknames. 'Boring, Annoying Kate' was a pain in the arse, as was 'Madame Yawn'. There was a guy there who was perhaps, well, retarded. Fuck knows what he was studying. He had a really pronounced lisp and did a campus radio show where everyone would phone in with requests that he'd find difficult to pronounce. It disgusted me actually, the way I'd use up all my change doing that.

National Express coaches were a big part of my life in those days. At the end of a term I'd get a coach to London, then the nine-hour night coach all the way to Glasgow. Looking back, I can see that National Express must have been one of the few companies that didn't run criminal-record checks on employees.

If you ever meet somebody with three fingers, a swallow tattoo on his neck and a temper, there's a fair chance he'll have driven for them in the 1990s. Never argue with those guys. One time we were getting into Glasgow in the fog. The driver got lost and we ended up heading back out onto the motorway. Everybody was taking the piss. 'Take us round Hampden, driver, we don't want to miss anything on your sightseeing tour!' The driver stopped the bus and leapt up into the aisle. He looked just like Mike Reid, with some worrying-looking prison ink.

'Fucking shut it! If I hear one more word you'll all be making your own fucking way to the station!'

What happened next is a good illustration of why Glasgow has never produced any truly world-class diplomats. A man stood up with his palms held out in front of him in a gently, gently manner and said,

'Calm down … ya prick.'

Half asleep, we all had to walk up the side of the motorway to a bus-stop in Easterhouse.

I used to have to wait for ages in Victoria Coach Station on the return journey. It was Dickensian in those days, predators comfortably outnumbering victims. There was a smoky wee Turkish greasy spoon and your best bet was to nurse a few cups of coffee in there with the straps of your luggage looped around your ankle. If I had to wait during daytime I'd go over the road to the pub beside the station. This was always a certain way to get talking to a recently released convict. They get a bus voucher when they're released and they'd all be having a few beers waiting for their connection. I met loads of terrifying people there and, as you can imagine, a clear majority were Scottish.

I remember seeing them refurbishing that place years later and just laughing. It was getting turned into an up-market brasserie but there was no way they could possibly change the clientele. The minute they reopened, it was going to be full of maniacs and unsold ciabattas. I went in after it had opened and was shocked to find a crowd of middle-class trendies. How did they manage it? Four quid a pint.

I've always been drawn to people who live on the fringes of society, probably because there were a lot of points when I looked like I'd be joining them. At uni I used to go out drinking with a Scottish homeless lad I'd met through a friend. Basically, I was such a heavy drinker that nobody could keep up with me for more than a couple of days, so I'd have a whole pool of reserve drinking partners for when one of my regular buddies was resting their liver. I'd sometimes go and drink with this guy and his friends at some kind of halfway house they stayed in. The homeless get a bad press. Nobody ever mentions how incredibly friendly they are if you turn up at their hostel with quite a lot of wine.

I noticed something among the regulars that I never hear talked about much, but which seems really key to me. People's terror of their own disorganisation and can't-be-arsedness is why we can live in a society that is so shit to the homeless. Yes, homelessness often overwhelms people through no fault of their own but it's related to that part of us that puts things off, that doesn't return calls or pay bills on time. I know that sounds terrible but it's actually important I think. The fact that people see that side of themselves in homelessness is part of the reason that they try to ignore the homeless. In our workaholic culture we don't want to admit to feelings of disorganisation or boredom with our jobs and lives. We don't want to empathise, to admit that the economic game we are all playing could see us homeless too. I think that homelessness is making us ill as a society. You're not supposed to ignore starving people every day; we are built to empathise and trying to shut that bit of ourselves down daily is really bad for everyone.

I asked one guy at the hostel how he ended up there.

'Have you ever not paid a bill for a couple of weeks, or been supposed to phone somebody and put it off?'

I told him that of course I had.

'Ever put it off for five or six weeks? If you just don't pay the bill or return the call, eventually you'll be here.'

It's for this reason I hate *The Big Issue*. It seems that we looked at the homeless and decided that their problem was that they didn't have anything to sell. That's a real failure to understand the problem, the solution that would be proposed by any travelling salesman. I like the way Blair came in and went on about stamping out 'aggressive begging', something I don't think anybody had ever experienced. Now the streets are a slalom of *Big Issue* sellers and Charity Cunts.

Not only am I not interested in the World Wildlife Fund, Mr Charity Beggar, neither are you. You're hired by an agency to represent a different cause every week. Chirpy morons who think that being friendly and extroverted is all it takes to get ahead in life. Middle age is going to hit them like a shotgun blast to the chest. You want to see something really horrifying? Sign off on a direct debit with a Charity Beggar and watch the shutters come down behind their eyes. They're scanning the street for the next weakling. Really, these blank-eyed date rapists might as well be androids.

At some point in the first year of uni, I went into town to sleep off a crippling hangover on the beach. Turned out I'd picked Brighton's famous nudist beach. How did I find this out? Did somebody have the good grace to tell me? No, I woke to find myself surrounded by a group of naked old people, a sight that could have defaulted the hard-on of a rapist on ecstasy. I find naturism indefensible. If there's nothing wrong with naturism then how come I'm still banned from Euro Disney? People say the world would be a better place if everyone were naked all the time. A better place for whom? Rapists. Saying there's nothing weird about naturism is like saying there's nothing weird about an 80-year-old man's massive saggy ballbag. There are bizarrely formed deep-sea fish with see-through bodies and eyes growing out their arses that are less weird than an 80-year-old man's saggy ballbag. The only thing in the world that is weirder is an 80-year-old man's saggy ballbag during a game of badminton. So, there's nothing wrong about letting your 12-year-old daughter play ping pong in the nude? With a 56-year-old dentist – who's returning the ball without a bat?

I mean, I'd like to go about dressed as a Viking in my day-to-day life; but I don't because I'm aware that would make me a weirdo. But who's more likely to get arrested when going for a pint of milk: a Viking or someone with their cock out? It's an experiment I've carried out and I can tell you … it's both. Yet I've never heard of anyone being put on the Viking offenders' register. Naturists are after all nothing more than swingers, but the worst kind of swingers – swingers who are too cowardly to let themselves be fisted in a stranger's Jacuzzi.

Naturists make the argument that 'it's nothing we haven't seen before'. I'm sorry, but that's not true. Believe it or not I have never seen an eighteen-stone man's sweaty testicles rest on a ping-pong table. I have never seen a 75-year-old woman's arse splayed open as she retrieves her ball on the crazy-golf course. I don't want to see these women naked. They look like they've sat on roadkill. Why do they have to be naked, live, in front of me? Why can't you just take a naked photograph of yourself, put it on the internet and let me find it in my own good time. And trust me, I will find it.

Let's be honest though, the ugliness is the real problem. If naturist beaches were full of people who looked like models I'd be down there with a wheelbarrow full of Kleenex and a heat pad on my wrist. Even so, I bet these beaches have perverts jacking off everywhere. Walking through that sand must be like wading through Scott's Porridge Oats.

Anyway, I tried to ignore the naked people for a while. Then, sitting up (an effort), I tried to nonchalantly throw a pebble into the sea. It hit somebody hard on the arse. To be fair, he had a huge arse – I'd been aiming at the sea and I'd hit it instead, that's how big it was. The nudists all started to waddle towards me angrily like obscene penguins but luckily couldn't move too quickly over pebbles. I shall stop this memory now, as it's distressing me.

To make beer money, I'd give tours of the campus to visiting sixth formers and their parents. I'd lie as much as possible, telling them that the refectory was a centre for animal experimentation and that once a term everybody had to dress as inmates of a concentration camp while the tutors role-played our Nazi tormentors. Once I managed to shag one of the sixth formers, quite a result for a drunken wreck peddling lies for three quid an hour. Her mum was on the tour but I managed to separate them; a championship sheepdog would have been proud of that one. I didn't have any condoms so borrowed some from our corridor drug dealer, perhaps the only time I spoke to him. When I got back to my room I found he'd given me a pack of brutally ribbed black johnnies. She took it like I was fucking her with a shotgun.

In my second year my grant cheques were late again. One turned up right at the end of the final term and I almost died from alcohol poisoning in the summer holidays. Being skint meant I spent most of the second and third terms living on my friends' couch. It was a three-storey house with no detectable right-angles, in which we created a biblically disgusting mess. I know you've probably lived somewhere you consider to have been messy. Unless you distributed two large bags of shit across your living room with a rake, it wasn't as messy as this place. There was a carpet of old CD covers and empty food containers that swirled dangerously underneath us like a special effect in a movie about magic tramps.

My flatmates included a very tall, well-spoken Englishman called Richard, who was an enormous sexual pervert. He came downstairs one day and told me not to use the Hoover for a while because he'd fucked it. Another bloke who lived there was an enthusiastic man-child called Ollie. He was a nice guy but incredibly distracted, strangely naïve and he spoke in a bubbling, disbelieving way that made his voice sound like it was coming from a 4-year-old. That, and the fact that he said exactly the same kind of things as one. At the very end of the whole year it was just Ollie and I left in the house. We had literally no money and planned to get through the last week using a big bag of rice and some saffron cubes we had to flavour it with. I came home to find that Ollie had cooked the entire bag in a vast cooking pot, not realising that cooked rice goes off. There was about a stone of rice in there and some days, as we starved, we would sit round the pot at dinner time and laugh the hysterical weak laughter of the very, very hungry.

Strangely, the film *Easy Rider* dominated life in the house. A couple of the guys were really obsessed with it, because they loved the look of that period and the music. It was a real big thing in Brighton then, that whole late-Sixties vibe. Anyway, because I was often in the house skint, I have seen *Easy Rider* about thirty times. I've watched it backwards twice. I'd like to say that you notice new stuff every time, but all I actually noticed was that after about twelve times it makes you want to kill yourself.

There was a fucked up old telly in the living room. For some reason, when the picture would go it would respond quite well to someone jumping up and down on the floor. 'Bobby Gillespie Starjumps' we'd call them and we got quite good at gauging how many were required. The picture would start to loop and someone would say, 'Three Bobby Gillespie Starjumps' and we'd maybe play cards to see who had to do them, but it generally worked. When we moved out we took that telly into the back garden and smashed it to death with bricks.

We'd play cards to decide pretty much everything. Who had to make the tea, or go to the shops. Towards the end, the whole place was just a stinking armpit and we had to clean it up before moving out. We played cards to decide who did what. Nobody wanted to do anything, so we played an epic card game that lasted for about five days. Five days in which lesser men would have been cleaning the house. I finished last and had to do the dishes, which we had never, ever done. It was truly fucking disgusting, unidentified textures brushing against my hands in the water like obscene wee creatures of the deep. Jacques Cousteau would have shat himself at some of this stuff. Mushrooms were growing out of meals people had eaten months before. Like a man, rather than thinking I needed to be tidier in future, I reflected that I needed to work on my card playing.

My drinking took on a new regularity during my second and third year at uni. When I had money I'd like to just sit in the pub on my own during the day, get drunk and read. There's an insidious side to alcohol where people think it's a great social lubricant, which it can be in moderation. My experience is that people often use it to cocoon a part of themselves and it's ultimately a drug of isolation. It's a depressant and its effects are mainly concerned with bits of the brain it shuts down, not opens up. I remember reading an interview with George Best where the interviewer met him down a pub where he'd go every day to drink a few pints, read the papers and do the crossword. He'd get really annoyed at people coming up to say hello, even though it must have happened constantly, what with the whole being George Best thing. That's where drinking takes you ultimately – it's an isolating thing that we do socially. It's also a drug that allows us to show emotion, in a culture where we're not permitted to do that very much, so people get addicted for social and emotional reasons as much as chemical ones.

Nowadays there's so much fuss about binge drinking? I mean, what exactly is binge drinking? Isn't it what we used to call 'drinking'. We're told that people are 'binge drinking over periods of two or three days'. Surely that's what we used to call a weekend. I was reminded of the phenomenon passing through Kilmarnock recently. Youths rampaged through the town centre like they were in a zombie movie designed to promote tracksuits. I was getting a train home on a Saturday and all the Celtic and Rangers fans got off the incoming train from the matches they'd been at, formed an orderly group at one end of the station and had a punch-up. It was like a regular chore they had to get through. I know I never got far with my urban-planning course, but I've always thought that Kilmarnock was a good example of why you should always build a town around a river, rather than a bus station.

I used to read all the time while I was drinking – you absorb information quite well in that relaxed state. That's probably why a lot of alcos get into horse racing and so on – there's a slight drunkenness that's almost like a trance state for taking in information. Comedy has a lot do with absorbing stuff and regurgitating it. It's often to do with knowledge – blurting out the name of just the stupidest historical figure or comic-book character or fruit-based dessert. I think that's the reason a lot of comics are alcos or stoners, or, like me, have been both.

The next year I lived with some friends who were in a band. They weren't students, just really mental lads from Portsmouth. They were pretty nuts, doing the odd fuckyouishly confrontational live show, and generally seeming to be up for a bit of a fight. My grant didn't turn up again and I spent a month stuck in the house with their massive comic collections.

That was what really got me into comics in the way I am now. They literally had thousands of comics and, with nothing else to do, I hot-housed their entire childhood of energy beams and parallel worlds. It was worth being skint to live a whole other childhood, finding the old *Justice Society of America* and *2000 AD* and *Eightball* as my stomach growled in our freezing house.

I still think that comics are one of the quickest ways to encounter alternative ideas. If all you've done is watch mainstream media, or read the books that get publicity, comics will blow your mind.

That house was at the top of one of the steepest streets anywhere; Albion Hill it's called and on certain parts of the ascent you feel like Spiderman. I'd like to see Kate Bush try running up that fucking hill. Sometimes I'd just be too pissed or tired to get up the fucker and would crash on the couch of a friend who lived at the bottom. There was a single dilapidated bench halfway up, at exactly the point where you could have really used a tent and some oxygen.

I found uni a bit of a drag towards the end. I wasn't hugely interested in the course or in many of the people. I think university insulates people from the real world. I'm all for being insulated from the real world, but maybe not in the way a cultural-theory lecturer is. Maybe more in the way that Prince is insulated from it, with gymnastic superhero sex and endless praise. There was a real politeness to seminars and all the discussions felt slightly perfunctory. I could never shake the feeling that most people in my classes would never read any of this stuff – or even think about it – ever again in their lives.

I remember quite a left-wing academic having a go at a student for being late and the guy explaining that he didn't have the train fare and had to hitchhike in. The tutor just didn't believe him, saying that the train was only a couple of quid and everyone had a couple of quid. This tutor was a Marxist, but had forgotten sometimes people don't have a couple of quid to spare.

Actually, I was the student, and I did have money and I'd turned up deliberately late to avoid doing a presentation I hadn't done any work on. But I feel the point still stands.

I hitched quite a lot at uni. I'd like to say it wasn't frightening but it always, always was. One guy who regularly picked me up had a wooden hand and didn't seem to be in total control of his vehicle. He never spoke either, slaloming the five miles into uni in total silence. Recently I read that the economic downturn in Britain has led to an increase in hitchhiking – and an even bigger increase in sales of gaffer tape and spades.

Graduation went alphabetically and you had to sit through the whole weirdness of it. Seeing adults with their parents is intrinsically wrong and you couldn't help thinking that in an older, better world, by the time people were adults their parents ought to have been dead. I went to the trouble of getting a doctor's note saying I had a kidney infection so that I could leave after my name got called and sit getting wasted in the bar, watching though frosted glass as beaming young men and women waved goodbye to university and hello to jobs in Brighton's graduate graveyard telesales industry.

After I graduated, age 22, I got a job working for a mental-health agency. There was a big asylum closing down near Brighton and people were being re-housed in the community. To ease the transition, people like me who'd be doing support work in the homes worked in the old asylum, mostly just chatting to people and taking them out on the odd day trip. The asylum was pretty tatty and the patients' rooms were just hospital-style cubicles, beds with a curtain pulled round them. There was lino everywhere. Lino not just on the floor but five feet up the walls, saying this institution has some interesting situations involving shit.

Some of the staff had been there for twenty years and were crazier than the patients. There was an orderly who was a huge Cornishman, built like a wrestler. He'd turn up at 7.30 every morning and go into the patients' telly room. Then he'd push about ten of the chairs together to construct a makeshift double bed and go to sleep until lunch.

A lot of the patients should never have been there. They'd been sectioned in the 1960s for things like depression, low IQs and alcoholism. There were some real characters too. A particular favourite was a well-dressed old guy who'd come into the telly room most days with an old vinyl record under his arm. It was 'The Stripper', that old, faux-sexy tune they'd always play years ago when someone stripped in a comedy sketch. He'd put it on and do this really stiff dance to it, arms held tightly to his sides, leaning forward from the hips and making careful eye-contact with everybody in the room. People ignored him and tried to watch *Countdown* but there was a scratch in the record that meant it never stopped. It could turn into a real battle of wills.

Another old gent thought he was Superman. He wore a really tight three-piece suit and spoke in a bizarre series of winks, clicks and whistles. I was intrigued by his Superman delusion and sometimes asked him about it. He would deny it at first, but this turned out to be a ploy to protect his secret identity. Once I went to fetch him for lunch and he was standing on his bed with his arms stretched out flying. He gave me a click and a wink and said, 'Well, now you know!'

I'd work in community houses too. It was great to see some of those people I'd got to know in that horrible hospital coming out and living in lovely suburban houses. I'd cook meals, clean, do the washing-up. All stuff I'd rarely do in my own house so I liked the novelty. I really enjoyed the nights when I had to sleep over; I'd sit up late with everybody watching TV and smoking and telling me their crazy life stories.

Sometimes I'd take people out to places they wanted to go. There was a little catatonic bloke called Brian who I'd take to the pub. He would never say a word. Sometimes he'd stare down at the table but occasionally he'd look up and smile, like he wanted me to talk. I'd sit there and talk to him about anything I could think of: football, politics, people I knew. When he was in the mood he'd just sit there and nod happily.

One guy wanted to go to church on a Sunday and Brian came down too. This guy was an elderly schizophrenic but also had something a bit like Tourette's. He'd often say pretty inappropriate stuff, always in a high-pitched chirping voice. The Church of England service is incredibly similar to the Catholic one, with the same fruity robes and hats. I can't understand the Anglican Church being so down on homosexuality. If you don't like gays, stop acting so gay. As the service started he launched into a refrain that he was to keep up for the whole thing. 'The vicar's bald. I've got a penis!' he said, loudly and relentlessly. After about an hour of this Brian looked up at me. It was the first time I'd ever heard him speak.

'This bloke is fucking nuts!' he said ruefully.

There's an interesting theory that madness is part of an evolutionary strategy. Diseases that are harmful are something that we generally evolve a resistance to. Madness has gradually increased, perhaps because the associated creativity is helpful to the species as a whole. Clearly, this is a theory devised by someone who never worked in a care home where they'd have to spend a significant part of an evening persuading an old man in his pants not to eat a family-sized block of cheese.

Occasionally patients would do a runner. Just walk away and keep going. One day Brian went missing for a wee bit. 'How far could he get?' I thought. He walked with a bit of a shamble and I'd never seen him move quicker than, say, a zombie. Turned out he had form and had once made it to Watford, where someone found him sitting at the side of the motorway with his shoes all worn out. This time he turned up at the bottom of the garden, thank God. I heard recently that a psychiatrist is running a trial to fit OAPs suffering from dementia with satellite navigation devices. If they want to give the elderly their freedom and dignity back they should do what we did for our granddad and fit them with a retractable leash. It sounds cruel but he never got lost or had an accident after that. Mind you, he never suffered from dementia either.

While I was working at the mental-health agency I lived in a big, shared house with a bunch of strangers. I think I just met a dodgy landlord in a pub and he gave me a room there. It was three guys working in graduate graveyard jobs in telephone sales. They were all ridiculously ambitious and committed to their horrifying company, and talked upbeat business bullshit. My kitchen of an evening was like a prototype of *The Apprentice*, my soul withering inside me as they presented tales of minor sales triumphs. Between them they possessed the moral value of a cat. It did mean I had the house to myself, because their employer had them working unpaid overtime and they were always sweating about some target or appraisal.

No doubt these guys have now all had their jobs outsourced to India. It always amused me that India didn't get the one telephone industry where we really could do with Indians on the phone. The Samaritans would benefit greatly if we had people on the line in Mumbai providing context for our trivial depressions.

You'd certainly have difficulty explaining your anxiety about having your in-laws over for Christmas to a guy who'd just watched his family being swept away in a flood.

I was one of those people you sometimes meet in care work who are quite fastidious about looking after their clients, but struggle to look after themselves. My fridge was like an 'Expert Level' episode of *Ready, Steady, Cook* ('Let's see what Frankie can make with an egg and some Lucozade'). I never bothered to get a duvet and slept in a sleeping bag, and for some reason had decorated my room with garden gnomes. My employers liked me though because I was always keen to do sleepovers. Other people didn't like those because they had lives and families. I just had a really shit house.

One day one of my flatmates had a day off at the same time as me. I could hear him downstairs playing music and knew I wouldn't be able to leave the house without having a long, harrowing conversation with him. I did what any reasonable person would do and shinned down the drainpipe. Hats off to the East Sussex police. They got a call about a burglar and had apprehended me before I got to the end of my street. I explained that I'd just been trying to avoid my flatmate and they frog-marched me back there so he could verify my story. He stood in the doorway, apparently unmoved, as I explained that I disliked him so much I had jumped out of a first-floor window. The police shuffled off looking embarrassed enough for all of us.

I have to say I've met some really decent coppers. Robert Anton Wilson is a writer who wrote a bunch of great books about freeing your mind. One of his first exercises is a little list of dogmas you should try to challenge yourself with. One of them is 'a cop, is a cop, is a cop'. It was hard to get my head around at first because as kids we were terrified of the police. I have a really vivid memory of walking with my mum while a teenager was hauled past surrounded by half a dozen officers. He was stiff with fear, held between two of them like a surfboard. Turned out he'd stolen a bottle of lemonade from a delivery lorry. A bold move, as it had been making a delivery to the police station. But at least he wasn't at one of the G20 protests. Have you seen the YouTube video of the protestor being assaulted by police officers? It's like a deleted scene from *The Lord of the Rings*. I keep expecting the camera to pan up to show the burning eye of Sauron glowing above the Bank of England. Eyewitnesses say she was definitely provoking the officer before she was assaulted. She's lucky she wasn't totally innocent otherwise she'd have gotten seven bullets in the head. The police officer hit her with a baton after she shouted 'I'm a woman!' at him. It's almost as if he thought she was reminding him – 'Oh yes, the small ones, they have weak legs, thanks for the tip.' These were the officers most highly trained to deal with incidents like this. What the hell were the untrained ones doing? Headbutting clergymen?

At least the video footage taken during the G20 protests proves that the police aren't prejudiced. They don't discriminate against hitting anyone, be they male or female, protestor or man on the way home from work. In every report that described the clashes with police the word 'apparently' was used before the word 'hit'. This suggests an element of doubt as to whether or not people were actually hit, as if there might be a chance that the videos are being played in reverse by mistake and could actually show the police helping people up off the ground with Velcro-covered batons. That whole scandal made me angry. The internet's got so many clips of policemen beating people up, it's a nightmare finding any porn.

Once the asylum closed completely, I got bored of the care in the community element of the job. I was just taking old people round charity shops and to the Bingo. To be honest, if you do that eight hours a day you start to smell stale urine everywhere.

I got a place doing a teacher-training course in Edinburgh. Like most people who go into teaching I was there because I couldn't think of anything else to do. There's a real irony that just as teenagers reach their most cynical and judgemental they are sent to be educated by a bunch of people who are there because they have failed at life. Lots of people were there because their parents were teachers. The police are a bit like that too. There's a good point made about all this by Grant Morrison, who says that Britain has a bit more of a caste system than it realises.

I hate the way that education gets used as a political plaything. What was that thing recently? Teaching British values in school? That's one step away from the prime minister throwing on a general's uniform and having a missile parade. 'And

Brown's popularity has soared since he unveiled his pet python.' School needs to be made more relevant to young people. They should test them on subjects that will come in useful – how to roll out of your kidnappers' moving car, blowjobs and maybe dungeon maintenance.

A recent report said that one in five teenagers self-harm. They could do with a good slap, but that's just playing into their hands. And Gordon Brown announced he wants to eradicate child poverty and stop child prostitution. Make your mind up! Young people are dying in our streets and this surely means there are questions we should be asking ourselves. Questions like what happens to all their iPods? Do the police get to keep them or is there an auction? There is talk of having 16-year-olds eligible to be those support police guys. What are they called? I simply don't care enough to find out. 16-year-old police? Do their powers include making a gun with their fingers and threatening to get their dad? Hiring teenagers sends out a message to community-support police everywhere. Basically their employers are telling them that they are only in a job because they haven't yet finalised training monkeys to take over. The minute they can get them to stop crapping in their helmets, you guys are out on your ear. I seriously think that teenagers are now the only people who can handle the police drinking culture.

I've always had a real problem with secondary education. It seems to exist to teach conformity and obedience over anything else. For me, it's all in the bell. The bell goes and you move along to the next class. It doesn't matter what you're learning about, it could be *Hamlet* or dark matter. That bell goes and you trot along because nothing is more important than the system.

My course qualified me to teach English and was full of the sort of boring, conformist bastards that made Hitler's rise to power so easy. I thought this was terrible at first, then once I'd been in some staffrooms I realised that these tedious flesh puppets were going to fit in perfectly. I always got on fine with the kids in schools; it was the teachers I struggled with. People who wear tweed and eat their lunch out of Tupperware might have things to tell your children, but those things are going to be thumpingly dull.

After years of thinking about it, it was during teacher training that I finally started doing comedy, aged 23. The Stand had a comedy club in the basement of W. J. Christie's bar in Edinburgh. Plonked at one end of a strip-club area known as the 'pubic triangle', it was run by Tommy Sheppard and Jane McKay, a couple so much larger than life they would have been scarcely believable if they'd turned up in Dickens. Tommy described himself as 'a businessman', which I later discovered is a Scottish synonym for 'crafty'. Jane compered the club and was always outrageous, hilarious, emotional and drunk.

I just turned up one night with a bunch of mates and asked if I could do a spot. Tommy told me that I'd have to book a spot and that obviously I couldn't just turn up and go on. I was disappointed and told him I'd come down with about ten people and we'd all have bought tickets. That changed things completely and he stuck me on for five minutes. It was a tiny little room holding maybe thirty or so, with a bar at one side, a dressing area in the fire escape and a mirror high above the bar. From the stage you could see your own face in the mirror, desperately trying to keep it together.

It went really well, even though my act was rubbish. Everybody starts off rubbish; it's a lot to do with trial and error, so how could they not? I think I started with some joke about how I'd like to know if I was going to be murdered so I could go around behaving really strangely for a few days just to mess up the reconstruction on *Crimewatch*. For the first year my act was all jokes about murders and people losing their legs and stuff like that. An ignored insight into what teacher training was doing to my sanity.

I hadn't really planned to go back but Tommy and Jane turned up at my halls of residence and stuck a postcard under my door telling me to get in touch. Within months I was compering the club drunk and they were my surrogate family. There was a regular techie, Chris Cooper, who was a frighteningly degraded-looking 26. He looked like a 26-year-old man from the Middle Ages and spoke in a low, rasping, sexualised whisper. There was a general Man Friday called Mac – a young artist who liked drinking, as opposed to speaking. The whole crew who formed around the place was bonded to it by their love of the club and much greater love of alcohol, drugs and sex.

I quickly learned that there are two types of comedian. The outgoing extrovert performers, they tend to hang around after the show and try to pull women from the audience. And then there

are the quiet, introverted comedians who have wives and families. They tend to shag the barmaids. Over the years the Stand
grew to have two full-time clubs – they're the best in the country,
one in Glasgow, one in Edinburgh. I was to form an almost
symbiotic relationship with the clubs' bar staff. I'd often go down
to hang out with them after shows, as they never came to the
actual show, preferring the company of those who were as jaded
and disgusted by stand-up as I was. I depended on the bar staff
to get me drugs, and I tried to pump as many of them as I could.
If you were to meet the concept of comedy bar staff on the astral
plane it would be represented as a giant, drug-encrusted orifice.
That didn't laugh at your jokes. Anyway, I can't diss comedy bar
staff too much; they've been good friends to me over the years.
And who knows, maybe I'll need to shag some more of them in
the future.

Coming up to the Edinburgh Festival in that first year, it was
decided that the Stand would run every night of August so as
to 'steal a march' on the festival proper. By the time the real
thing kicked off we'd done eight nights in a row and were
possibly in the advanced stages of alcohol poisoning. I was so
bored that I started going through the bins outside the venue to
find stuff to talk about. I'd come on wearing discarded specs
I'd found in the rubbish and do half the show through an old
picture frame.

Edinburgh itself has always felt a bit inauthentic to me. Like the
shortbread-tin side of ourselves we use to attract American tourists.
To be fair, the Americans do make great comedy audiences during

the festival – always whooping and cheering. I often think that we should be more heavily medicated as a society. I think it's every patriotic Scot's duty to help out American tourists. Latch onto them and let them know about your city:

'This is Princes Street. So called because it's owned by the pop star Prince. Here, on Calton Hill, there are all kinds of night-time events and they're all free! It's where they held the auditions to find the Bay City Rollers. And here we have Scott's Monument. Erected to honour James Doohan who played Scotty in *Star Trek*. If you go all the way to the top, there's an animatronics model of Lieutenant Uhura reading the Federation Charter. Well worth the climb. This statue of Greyfriars Bobby is the actual dog, who was so overcome with grief when his owner died that he threw himself into a cement mixer. This is John Knox's house – where he lived before he went off to present *Blue Peter* with Shep.'

Tommy decided to start selling luxury filled rolls at the shows. Probably a bit of a surprise to anybody who'd staggered into a dingy basement near a strip club, largely so they could keep drinking, to be confronted with a choice between Gruyère and French mustard. Tommy became preoccupied with roll sales. How the shows were doing actually became something of a side issue. One night Mac and I started giving away the rolls to the local homeless, who couldn't understand what any of the fillings were.

'Brie and avocado!' offered Mac to a baffled tramp. '… That's eh, cheese and eh … well, avocado.'

Tommy was enraged when he found out. 'To the homeless! To the fucking homeless?!' I managed to pacify him by pointing out that he was Deputy General Secretary of the Scottish Labour Party and he saw the funny side.

A highlight of that period was Tommy's appearance on *Masterchef*. The show would always do a wee bit of back story with the guests, and Tommy wanted to be thought of as the sort of person who went on country walks with Irish setters. He wasn't; he was the sort of person who liked to get drunk and sleep late, so he had to scour Edinburgh for dogs to borrow and persuade Jane to be filmed climbing a hill with them. I watched it drunk and felt like I was looking into a weird new dimension. Everyone used to give their dishes fancy French names but Tommy – a dour bastard but still the most cheerful person ever to come out of Ulster – called his things like 'Pie and Veg'. Gordon Ramsay was the judge and panelled him. This was in the days before Ramsay was allowed to swear, although he looked like he really wanted to.

My drinking certainly seemed to be a lot less out of place in Scotland. Good old Scottish drinking. Other nations think of us as the great party nation. Oh no, that's Ireland; and they think of us as kind of depressed. I found that I was drinking more and more, and my behaviour was becoming more extreme. Living in the part of the Venn Diagram where 'Scottish People' meets 'Comedians', nobody noticed. A key skill for alcoholics is to be able to make light of vomiting. 'I think I was an asset to that barbeque ... burp.' Once I woke up in Tommy and Jane's and found that I couldn't see. Eventually, I realised that this was because I wasn't wearing my glasses. I had a tribal memory of vomiting out of a window, so I looked out of the window in the living room. There, two floors below, my glasses stood face-up in a puddle of vomit being eaten by a seagull. That served as a sort of wake-up call and five years later I quit.

My main teaching placement was at a school in Muirhouse. It's quite a deprived part of Edinburgh, near where *Trainspotting* is set. It was a community high school with really brilliant kids. My principal was an amazing woman called Margaret Hubbard, who pioneered media studies in Scotland and was really insistent on teaching kids to question who produced what they were watching and why. She toured primary schools with a class that taught kids to decode children's programmes. It was called 'The Ideology of *Postman Pat*'. She was great. The kids told me that occasionally her back gave out and she'd teach them while lying down in the middle of the floor.

Working in that area gave me a real sense of how marginalised a lot of folk are; how completely not invited to the party. Life there wasn't terrible but a lot of stuff should have been a lot better. A couple of the kids walked me round their area one day, showed me where they hung out, and it just made me really furious at what the world was offering to them. The place was full of nice, spirited kids and their country just didn't seem to give a fuck about them.

I had to recalibrate my expectations of the children a bit too. A bunch of the first-year guys started talking to me one day about the actress Isla Fisher, who was in *Home and Away* at the time. 'Ooh, do you fancy her then?' I asked, in the teasing manner I remembered my own uncles employing with me. 'Got a wee crush on her?' One of them looked up at me baffled, and blinked, 'Sort of, Sir. Eh, it's more that we'd all like tae ride her.'

I spent free periods and lunchtimes with the other students on placement. They were three women who were all beautiful in totally different ways, all immaculately dressed in skirt suits from Next. This led to me teaching many of my classes in a disembodied state of sexual reverie. Once, while my second years were reading a poem, I was only brought back to reality by the sound of my own grinding teeth.

I was never much of a teacher. There were often times when the complete unreality of the whole thing hit me. I'd see myself standing writing at a blackboard like somebody's teacher. I was somebody's teacher! It wouldn't have been a whole lot weirder if I'd quantum leaped into the body of a 1950s housewife. There were only a couple of kids who were really unbearable. I sat them together so that if I felt the need to fart I could walk casually by their table. Kids never really think of teachers as farting, so they'd go absolutely nuts at each other.

There was a wee guy in my third year who was unbelievably gay. Well, maybe not actually gay but certainly destined for gayness. Once, I set that class a short story and got the usual selection of stuff about scoring the Cup Final winner for Hibs or Hearts, winning the lottery and so on. He produced this tempestuous forty-pager about a woman trying to make her way in the fashion industry of Milan. She was designing a collection on a shoestring while her Cuban ex-lover attempted to blackmail her for sex. He succeeded actually. He 'inserted himself inside her' in a shower, in the one scene that the author's heart didn't seem to be in.

At the end of that placement there was a school talent show. I did my stand-up act. I'd been going for maybe six months then, so I was alright at it. The place was packed out with kids and former pupils. It was a really wild gig, playing to little kids who responded like a drunken crowd on a Saturday night. You haven't lived until you've done a putdown on a 13-year-old boy from your form class. Obviously, it was about him being a virgin. He'd probably had more sex than me.

I couldn't stand most of the students on the English teaching course so I'd hang out with three or four bad hats. Living in halls with people who aspired to teach physical education was fairly wearing on the soul and I was really looking forward to the course finishing.

I hated it at the time, but I think I'd find teacher training unbearable now, especially as bankers are being encouraged to go into teaching. Can you imagine a banker in the school room? 'OK, so let me demonstrate. I have no apples and you have thirty apples. You give me all your apples. So I have all the apples. HA HA HA LOSERS! I HAVE ALL THE APPLES! SCUM!' Before taking a pension of four million apples.

Some schools are hiring bouncers to control disruptive pupils when teachers are off sick and supply teachers are brought in.

Classes are a lot better behaved now that pupils are barred from getting in for wearing trainers, and ugly kids are being sent to schools around the corner.

My final placement was a wash-out. The department didn't want a student there and actually stopped speaking to me. I enjoyed that immensely, often going up to the other teachers and telling them the whole psychedelic plot of a Michael Moorcock book I was reading while they attempted to ignore me. It involved a parallel 1970s earth where the British Empire spanned the whole globe with the aid of giant Zeppelins. The only guy who spoke to me was a predatory homosexual. I finally worked out the key phrase that would make him go away. It turned out to be, 'I think that you are a predatory homosexual.'

So with nowhere else to finish the final placement, I got put into a primary school for a month or so. Primary teaching isn't a real job. Getting children to make paintings out of seashells and glitter? That's pretty much what they'd do if you weren't in the room. Also, you don't need to know that much. Just tell them loads of lies and they'll believe you. I fought against the temptation to tell them that face-painting was invented by the Jews during the war to hide from the Nazis. 'You are mistaken, Herr Kommandant! We are not Jews! We are TIGERPEOPLE ... except him, he's Spiderman.'

Nowadays, the curriculum in primary schools is to be revamped so that children are familiar with blogging, podcasts, Wikipedia and Twitter. Aren't kids already familiar with all of these? The average primary-school child is already more relaxed with computers than a NASA scientist. Talk about putting a strain on the teachers. The only people qualified to teach children aged 7 about how the internet works are children aged 8. Another problem with this revamping is that information technology is moving so quickly that by the time children leave school, websites like Twitter will be as dead as the dodo. Although pupils won't have been taught what a dodo is; they'll be saying 'as dead as MySpace'. Teaching children about information technology is going to replace fad activities, such as reading books and learning about history. That might seem like a dreadful shame to us, but remember that future generations are going to have to fight the cyber wars and, unfortunately, knowing how to download plans for an electromagnetic pulse disruptor is going to be more useful to them than knowing how long Queen Victoria reigned when they come face to face with an army of giant robotic bees.

Actually, my primary-school placement was a great time for me. Everybody was incredibly tolerant of having an idiot, who couldn't paint or draw, lumber round their classrooms trying to show them how to paint and draw. During the weekly assembly when hymns were sung, I had to sit outside with a wee Jehovah's Witnesses boy whose parents didn't want him to take part for religious reasons. Those were great afternoons: a hundred tiny voices singing to Jesus while this little lad with bottle-top specs questioned me incessantly about my life in the outside world.

He said that I should see him throw a cricket ball. I've since discovered that this is an almost genetically innate ability some people have. Ian Botham held the world record for years and then I think it passed to Ian Botham's son. Anyway, I wasn't really supposed to but one day when everybody was singing hymns I got hold of a cricket ball and we sneaked out to the field behind the school. There wasn't a house for about half a mile. I can still see him launching it like a fucking rocket towards the horizon, beaming up at me as glass broke in the distance. We gave each other that man-shrug that says, 'Nobody needs to know about this. Let us never speak of it again.'

I'd been going out with a girl since working in mental health, and after I finished teacher training we got married. Why? I was drunk. I was drunk for the courtship, proposal, wedding and most of the year-long marriage itself. I know that I should probably em and ah a few regrets here but, to be honest, drunkenness is quite a good way to approach marriage. Relationships are largely about blotting out other people's failings, having an idealised version of somebody to relate to. It's so much easier not to notice those failings when you can't see your own face in a shaving mirror and sleep like a well-fed hamster. Fuck it, I tried. Oh no, wait a minute. I didn't.

I read recently that the secret to a happy marriage is for a man to marry a woman who's far more attractive than him. This is according to the results of a scientific investigation carried out by … a really ugly scientist. This is the follow-up to his earlier studies, 'Why scientists should mate with supermodels' and 'Why men with tiny cocks make the best lovers.'

During the marriage we lived in Bromley. It's in Kent, but is really a suburb of London. Basically, if you ever have to go there and you really can't get out of it, kill yourself. I'd kill myself if I had to change trains there. Nobody between the ages of 18 and 30 lives there; only the occasional acid casualty living with their parents will have failed to get the fuck out at the first opportunity. It's so incredibly nondescript that I would feel foolish trying to describe it. Avoid.

We had a dog, a little cocker spaniel. As I only worked doing stand-up at weekends, I spent a lot of time with the dog, until I found that I was starting to look and behave like a dog. One day I shaved off all its fur and arranged it in the shape of the dog on the living-room floor, even putting its little collar on. When my wife came home I pretended it had been in an accident and she burst into tears. I still have no idea why that relationship didn't work out. That dog will be dead now. I'm talking about the spaniel, rather than my ex-wife. I read that the world's oldest dog just turned 21. It's a dachshund and it struggles to see, hear and walk. That's not really a dog is it? That's a draft excluder that shits itself.

Paul Marsh lived in Bromley at the same time and so we got to hang out a bit. A typical evening involved Paul renting a video that he thought looked good. To me the same video would look like it had been made as a satirical joke about creativity entropy. He would then lose interest in it during the first ten minutes and play his guitar really badly as I watched in rapt horror. Pretty much anything that would normally dissuade you from renting a film will encourage Paul to get it. It's British? Cool. It's been directed by Keith Allen's brother? Yes please. It features a lingering nude shot of an elderly Michael Caine? Give me two. In this, as in so many other ways, Paul has often made me wonder if he is an alien trying to work out what's normal. There's a key phrase that I'll say one day that will make him think that his cover's been blown and he'll have the whole planet incinerated with a few incomprehensible words into his shirt-cuff microphone.

I just couldn't be arsed getting a teaching job and just drifted into doing comedy full time. I had a contract to do a thing called 'The Comedy Network', which was basically a whole load of university gigs. These were incredibly variable. One night you'd be playing packed gigs to 500 people in a theatre set-up, the next you'd be standing in a corner of a freezing bar talking to one table of baffled foreign students. To be honest, it was usually the latter.

My first tour was with Paul Sneddon doing his Vladimir McTavish act, which confusingly is not a character. I compered and the other act was Seán Cullen, doing a character called Dame Sybille. He was an old lady of the English theatre relating bizarre and almost entirely improvised anecdotes about her life in show business. It didn't matter how unpromising the room or the crowd looked, he would improvise almost the entire thing, even though the character had a lot of funny stock lines. He was unbelievably gifted. One particularly grim-looking group, which comprised a handful of science students and the venue bouncers, got treated to a bizarre treatise on Dame Sybille's life among the Native American Indians. She had been a Dr Moreau-like figure among them and had, for some reason, bred a race of horses with human hands. It ended with a thrilling denouement where the Indians turn against Dame Sybille and she climbs up a large rock only to hear the horses with their human hands climbing up behind her. The Chief confronts her at the top but says nothing; he simply makes his horse stand on its hind legs and slap her in the face.

There was a gig in Newcastle where they put all the acts up in a flat for a few nights while they worked over the weekend. One morning, this comic got up and told us all about this terrible nightmare he'd had. He'd been booked to do a show in a pub somewhere but there was no stage so he had to stand on bales of straw but there was no microphone, so he just had to shout as people talked at the bar. I pointed out that we'd all done much worse gigs than this in real life. When we got talking, it turned out one guy had done a show standing on top of a car in a car showroom during the day, as people walked by trying to gauge if he was a schizophrenic. Another bloke had done a gig where he turned up only to be bundled into a van and driven up to a group of a dozen elderly people in a car park. The van reversed towards the crowd and the back doors were flung open – him standing slightly hunched in the back doing his act.

I've got my own share of horror stories. There used to be a festival in Glasgow called Mayfest and there was some kind of bylaw that if pubs put on entertainment that wasn't music they would get a late licence for free. I suppose the idea is that boozers would stick on scenes from *Death of a Salesman* and people would be culturally enriched as they got drunk and gubbed handfuls of dry roasted peanuts. In practice, bar owners stuck on stand-up to exploit the loophole. You'd have to do five minutes so they could get their licence, but it paid £50 and you could do a few in a night. I did one in a big converted church on the South Side. There were about 300 people in on a Saturday night. The DJ just went, 'Here's a comedian' and handed me his mic, which was tethered to the mixing deck by about two feet of cord. I crouched there and did some jokes and everybody seemed to be laughing uproariously, albeit slightly in the wrong places. When I got off, one of the punters explained that everybody was laughing at a laser that somebody had centred on my forehead, making it look like I was in the sights of a sniper's rifle.

The worst gig I did was one in the Harbour Arts Centre in Irvine. There had been a music festival on somewhere during the day and they just let all the festival-goers in for free. The organiser looked out into the room and gave me this little satisfied nod. It was like she was saying, 'If there's one thing I like to see before a gig, it's bodies swaying and lurching around the room like a challenging level in a zombie game.' She got up and for some reason tried to do a raffle, then it was me. I think I tried a putdown on some heckler and he just walked up onto the stage and started screaming – it was a comprehensive emotional breakdown of some kind. There was actually foam on his mouth and I just stood there and watched him, suddenly completely bored. I managed to get him to sit down just by pointing wordlessly at his empty chair, like he was a trained animal. In reality, this cunt could only dream of the education that had been lavished on a good sniffer dog. It was hopeless. I managed to get a bit of hush, then said, 'You people need to get yourself a fucking karaoke machine', dropped the mic and walked off through this booing mob.

What I'd forgotten was the rider. I got outside and then had to walk calmly back through the crowd to get the box of booze from the dressing room. People were going nuts, screaming in my face and stuff. Fuck it, I was going to need to drink if I was staying in Irvine. I was staying next door in the B&B and so, it turned out, was a lot of the audience. I woke up the next day, having drunk the rider, to see that I had piled all the furniture in the room against the door to thwart their efforts to get in there and kill me. I had no memory of what must have been a reasonably challenging evening. Good old booze.

I'd recommend that everybody try bombing on stage at least once. People are always chasing new highs; what about new lows? I can assure you that dying on your arse is a low you won't believe. I heard of a guy who died during a benefit gig for victims of miscarriages of justice. An old guy came up and put his arm round him at the bar. He felt a bit better until he realised that he had done so badly he was being commiserated with by one of the Birmingham Six.

I played for a big chain of clubs called Jongleurs for a bit. They'd only book me for their easier clubs and always put me on first. I loved that. I'd have hated to get any more work from them; there wasn't a moat and chicken wire across the front of their stages but you felt it would have helped sometimes. They were really strict about everybody doing twenty minutes. I was terrified that they'd promote me to their rougher venues or to headlining the ones I was doing, so I always did as short a set as possible. In fact, if I thought it was going too well I'd stop doing jokes and just chat about my day for a bit.

There was a rough venue I'd compere a lot called The Frog and Bucket, in Manchester. It's on a really rough street, the sort of place you'd go to hire a hitman. Once I got mugged when I was going down there. Two junkies grabbed me; they both had knives but I managed to somehow wriggle free and get to the front door of the club. They had some truly startling security at that club and even in the midst of the shock of it all, I laughed to see some full-on maniac of a doorman with a telescopic truncheon run off up the road looking for the guys.

'Gig on the Green' was a festival that used to be on Glasgow Green in the summer. An interesting part of town, it meant that there was a broad mix of studenty, music-loving types and people who were there to rob them. I turned up and the tent was packed with people waiting for the compere Phil Kay, who is hugely loved in Scotland for being an unpredictable genius and maniac. Phil was late and the organiser just wanted me to go straight on, but I got them to hold it for a bit. Eventually, Phil turned up and just walked straight on to this huge, football-ground roar. The first thing you could hear as it died down was one of the crowd shouting, 'Show us your dick!' Phil immediately replied, 'I'll show you it if you get up here and wank it for me!' and actually got it out. There was a big gasp from the crowd and this bloke, fair play, decided he was going to honour his commitment to get up there and wank it for him. Realising he'd need some momentum to get past security, he sprinted right at the stage and was in the middle of an impressive leap as two bouncers intercepted him and drove him face first into the ground like a fencepost. All I could hear through the chaos was '… please welcome Frankie Boyle!' I shook hands with Phil as I took to the stage, trying not to look at his exposed penis.

A weird side of stand-up is that you get to spend a lot of time in places that nobody ever goes. You wait to go on in corridors filled with beer barrels, or rehearse on fire escapes outside venues. The same is true of the places you go to on your way there – the motorway services, the coffee shops in railway stations. I'm probably one of the only people in the country who knows this, but Leicester station has the most purgatorial café in the UK. It has the usual depravity of fruit machines and Formica tables but seasons it with a set of framed photos running all around the walls of famous people who come from Leicester. Gary Lineker, he's from Leicester. So is David Attenborough and the snooker player Willy Thorne. The fact that none of these people chose to stay in Leicester is irrelevant. So what if they thought that it was better to move away from Leicester? The final face is Joseph Merrick, the Elephant Man. It says a lot when a town takes pride in being the birthplace of a hugely deformed circus freak. Even he pissed off to London. And it's not even him; it's a photo of John Hurt in the movie. The UK's National Space Centre is in Leicester, because proximity to the town gives scientists an added incentive to come up with technology to get off the planet.

Dope smoking is similar to stand-up in that way. You get to see a lot of unusual psychogeography, smoking joints in alleyways and on patches of waste ground. I remember once getting stoned behind an old tumbledown wall in a Glasgow park and thinking that I probably had my own name in the language of the local stray cats. Another time there was a murderer on the run in Glasgow and every time I went for a joint I'd panic, thinking 'If I was a murderer this is exactly where I would hide!'

Travelling around Britain as a stand-up I really noticed how public space has been colonised. Every park or public garden seems to be seen by councils as a missed opportunity to sell lattes and Cornettos. I remember reading some Scottish politician bemoaning the fact that Loch Lomond attracted hordes of visitors but didn't have anything for them to buy. They built a big shopping centre on the banks and of course nobody shops there. Because it's a shopping centre and they've turned up to see a fucking lake. I hate that attitude of wondering how you can make things pay. It's a sickness. Queuing in a railway station to pay 30 pence to take a piss makes me feel like a shambling animal in an abattoir. And Ryanair have recently announced that they are going to charge passengers to use their toilets, although they seem to prefer it when people refer to them as planes. A pound to go to the loo on their planes?! Michael O'Leary has obviously never eaten his own airline food. How long before he installs coin meters in the chairs just to keep the plane flying?

Another thing I soon learned from my early days on the road is that a tiny but determined minority of stand-ups are compulsive liars. Everybody knows who these guys are and most people really look forward to car journeys with them, just for the sheer, wild, Michael Moorcockesque unreality of it all. There was one guy who told me that he was a black belt in aikido, but had to retire after cutting off his big toe with a sword. As he sat in front of me wearing sandals. He also told me a story about a friend of his who jumped off the Pompidou Centre in Paris into a bucket of water.

'You mean a tank of water …?' I replied.

'No, a bucket!'

'Like in a *Tom and Jerry* cartoon?'

'Yes.'

On a different occasion another guy went outside to take a mobile-phone call when we were sitting in the dressing room of Glasgow Jongleurs. The Rolling Stones were playing in town that night and of course this maniac said Mick Jagger was phoning to see if he could borrow a couple of local gags. In its own way, that's weirder than anything the Yorkshire Ripper did.

This same guy phoned me one time and asked if he could do a weekend I had booked in with a club up north because his wife was in hospital with cancer. Her hospital was near the venue and it meant he'd be able to be by her side. Why he'd want to be zipping off from the bedside to berate students for 120 quid a night I didn't know. Maybe they needed the money for cancer drugs or something? Of course it turned out his wife was absolutely fine, quite cheerful in fact, as she'd split up with him a couple of years before. It was worth losing the work because every time I met him for a few years after this I'd get him to update me on his wife's recovery. I really banged on about it incessantly. I think in the end he just told me she'd died. It's just like the lying kids at school; the stand-up circuit is a bit dull. Those guys think that the truth is a bit too boring to tell and they're sort of right. Mind you, comedians in general are such social retards. Every time I'm stuck in a dressing room I keep expecting Tom Cruise to turn up and drive them all to Vegas.

ELEVEN

Having been going full time on the comedy circuit for about a year, I did a run of gigs in Dubai. It's the only time I've ever done that sort of thing because I hate flying and I hate expats. There are only two reasons for someone becoming an expat. Either they've failed at life in Britain or they're a paedophile. The whole British expat community there is like the residue of some experiment to clone Jeremy Clarkson. It's full of people who can never come home because they get used to the maids and the deference. They always end up going on to other outposts of neo-colonial horror and their CVs read like they're the hero of a Joseph Conrad novel. When they come back, expats always say things like, 'I can't believe you still live here ...' and you know they're only ever a few drinks off saying, 'because of the blacks'. They always bang on about the weather and the food, like that's more important than the place being a Third World police state. Here's a wee rule of thumb I have (no doubt some people will find it naïvely idealistic): never live in a country that imprisons homosexuals.

The people putting on the gigs were really decent but it took me the first week to get over the flight. I've always hated flying, partly because I didn't get on a plane till I was in my twenties. I distinctly remember that first time as we roared up the runway thinking, 'If this thing goes any faster we're going to take off!' I'd take loads of Valium and sleeping pills for every flight for a while, but once I was so out of it that I seized a man on take-off and fell asleep with my arms around his neck. Perhaps I was trying to take him hostage, perhaps I'm a deeply sublimated homosexual.

The brace position they ask you to take up in the event of a crash (head between knees) is actually designed so that your teeth will stay with your corpse and they can identify the body. I reckon that if you time it just right at the moment of impact you can probably spit all your teeth into someone else's lap, messing things up for everybody.

I hate people who say, 'Don't worry, if you're in a plane crash it'll all be over in an instant!' That's the problem. I can't believe that people actually try to reassure you by saying that you're going to be snuffed out of existence in an instant of unimaginable pain. Those who tell you there's no such thing as a good way to die are people who have clearly never heard the phrase 'drug-fuelled sex heart attack'. On a plane going down you'd fuck anything. I hit an air pocket last week and I had half a mind to hump the trolley. That's why they never released the black boxes from 9/11. It's probably nothing but sex groans and the occasional, 'Blow this tower, Mustapha!'

I stayed in Dubai for a week or so and did a range of different gigs. Some were just like a nice club gig at home, some were like a shite gig in a pub in the Middle East. One was in an expat village – the sort of people who travel to another country and want to be surrounded by other British people, if you can imagine that. There's a thing that happens when you do shows where lots of people are sitting with their boss – they wonder if they're allowed to laugh. This was exactly like that, but there was a big Scottish group who were just visiting and didn't have to worry about whether anybody else approved. They were just killing themselves. It was great, most of the room just silent and twenty or so guys could hardly breathe. It was hugely uncomfortably, perversely enjoyable. It was the first time I realised I could totally split a room and still do well, that some people in crowds would always hate me but I didn't really need them anymore.

Everyone on the tour was a great laugh. One of the organisers was a forty-something woman and was trying to shag one of the acts, who was horrified. She was a nice woman but, well, looked constipated. One night it was just the three of us in a hotel room, so the guy kept up an intense conversation with me about movies, desperately hoping I wouldn't leave him alone with her. As I left, you could see real terror dawning. 'Wait a minute, Frankie!' he shouted desperately as I was closing the door. 'Do you remember that movie where Eric Stoltz played a boy with a giant face? Do you?!'

I'd never been anywhere sunny before so I loved it, just laughed the whole time. I wonder how much of our national temperament, and my own, is simply due to the pish weather. I actually have a policy not to do anything major in Scotland in the winter – everybody's in a terrible mood. A recent survey revealed that one in ten Scots are on anti-depressants, which begs the question, what have the other nine got to be so happy about? It also reported that people in Scotland are more depressed in the winter months but I think we just hate the fact that there are twelve of them. But the truth is no poll will ever truly reflect our national character, because no poll includes a category of choked alcoholic sobs. When I was a kid there was an old Spectrum game called *The Hobbit*. One of those old type-in adventures:

'Get the Sword!'

'I see no Sword here.'

'Take the Sword!'

'What Sword?'

'Pick up the Sword!'

'You take the Sword. The Orc Chief kills you.'

You'd always get stuck in the Goblins' Dungeon. For a while nobody could work out how to get out of there. You'd be sitting there for ages. After a long time (like a day or something) your character-friend Elrond would appear with a glassy look in his eyes, trying to kill you. That's how I think of Scotland in winter – the Goblins' Dungeon. People you know well will become unrecognisable after six months of rain. Sometimes you look into a set of glassy eyes and know they're only a short step away from cleaving your skull with one well-placed blow. I once did a pilot in Scotland at Christmas and it was like trying to lead a troop of depressed chimpanzees into battle.

I read recently that Andy Roddick challenged Andy Murray to a competition to see how long they could stay in an ice bath, and lost. Obviously Roddick forgot Murray is Scottish. Between October and March this whole country is basically one giant ice bath. At one point Murray actually broke into a sweat. If he'd challenged Murray to sit in a hot tub he'd probably have killed him.

My marriage fell apart quite quickly. I stopped drinking for about nine months and my wife didn't seem to like me when I was conscious. I left on a bus with all my stuff and went back to Glasgow, my life falling to bits behind me like a temple that's been robbed by Indiana Jones.

Tommy and Jane were off on holiday so I got to flat-sit their house for a bit, do some gigs and gradually piece my head back together. They had a flat in Marchmont and it was good to live the life of Inspector Rebus for a bit, walking round the Meadows, listening to their Seventies music and often popping out for a fish supper for my tea. The only rule they had was not to use their bedroom because I was still smoking at the time, and Tommy just hated the smell of smoke in his bedroom. One night, one of the barmaids from the Stand came back. She said quite casually that she had a boyfriend, so couldn't do anything sexual with me, but I could do whatever I liked to her. Encouraged, I made a pretty good effort at fucking her to death. She could have checked her fanny into a Women's Refuge. Of course, I had got the date of

Tommy and Jane's return wrong and they walked in to find me fucking one of their staff, in their bed, a lit cigarette smouldering in the ashtray.

After so many years in England I was really glad to be home. Devolution started the year I moved back, although I think nearly half of the electorate didn't vote in that election. That got written up as voter apathy. Quite typically, vainglorious politicians look at a statistic like that and think, 'What's wrong with people? Why don't they use their vote?' You never hear them asking, 'What's wrong with us? Why aren't we worth voting for?' It seems to me that if they want to get people excited, the SNP should play up the party element of independence. The slogan should be 'Independence – It'll be a hell of a night! Well, let's be honest, month.' Glasgow city centre will have streets running with rivers of whisky and blood, as drunken revellers spill their whisky into the long-standing blood rivers. Edinburgh will have millions of pounds' worth of fireworks, which on the stroke of midnight will be launched at head-height towards England. Aberdeen, as on every BBC Hogmanay, will be Stripping the Willow. I'm not convinced that this isn't just a tape that Aberdeen puts on for the rest of us while locally showing something which more closely reflects Aberdeen's real culture – like a porno version of *A Fistful of Dollars*. Dundee, of course, will be bedlam. Murders, rockets being fired into the sky … who knows when news of independence will manage to seep through?

My friend Scott had just got divorced as well. He decided that we should both go on holiday to get hammered and blow off some steam. Scott is a wonderful and hilarious human being. He's a theatre director and thus appears gay but isn't. I always find those guys to be like some jungle spider whose markings make them look like some kind of plant so they can lure insects. Much like the jungle spider, Scott had to make do with about one victim a year. Scott is always tense and slightly worried, always trying to quit smoking, always in some kind of slight distress – he's like a beautiful, bittersweet sitcom that never got made. He has, I should add, the most remarkably brown and crinkled face. Once I asked his baby daughter to describe him in three words. 'That's easy!' she replied. 'A paper bag!' One of his more endearing traits is a seemingly endless and original set of euphemisms he has for his own penis. There's a new one every day; 'The Kidney Wiper' was my favourite, until he came up with 'The Vomiting Milkman'.

Somehow Scott had managed to become quite well known as a director of youth theatre in Romania. I'm sure 'quite well known as a director of youth theatre in Romania' is used in many social circles as a synonym for 'paedophile', but Scott was actually incredibly talented at his job. He had some seminars to do while we were over but I was free to focus entirely on drinking colourless local liquids until I forgot my marriage or just shat a lung.

I got aboard the plane and started to put in some work towards getting drunk. Scott, it was clear from an emotional check-in, was in the grip of a crippling hangover and desperate for a drink. He sank a double vodka and the relief or shock or something made his leg shoot out involuntarily into the aisle, accompanied by a loud cry of pain mixed with triumph. It should have been clear then that the trip was going to be *Withnail and I in the Third World*.

We landed pissed and were met by our unflappable guide, Claudio. I stood at the carousel trying to recognise my luggage and still hadn't managed to form any kind of greeting. Finally I alighted on an ice-breaker.

'What would you say is the worst film ever made?' I asked, attempting to look him in the eye.

'*Clash of the Titans!*' he beamed back, like that was the first question everybody asked him.

At that time, Bucharest was full of stray dogs. It might still be full of them, I'm certainly not going back to the shithole to find out. The dogs lived in terror of the people, who exhibited a blasé brutality towards them. There was one town on the trip that didn't have a dog problem. The local mayor had promised to get rid of them in his election manifesto. When he got in he had them rounded up and fed to the lions in the local zoo. It's only when you go to Europe that you realise how unbelievably kind to animals the British are. The Romanian equivalent of *Pet Rescue* would feature a naked Rolf Harris running through a burning petting zoo with a club.

Scott had tried to prepare me for the shocking poverty, warned me how much of a psychic torpedo that could be. I laughed it off right up to the point where it triggered a near nervous breakdown. Old women washing their faces in puddles, a 5-year-old boy prostitute tottering towards our cab in high heels. One day we stepped out of our flat to see an old man on his knees pounding the pavement with a tiny hammer. We just cracked – laughed and laughed till we were nearly sick at the horror we had found there and the horror we had brought.

Scott could speak Romanian quite well, he told me, and would certainly throw himself into it. He'd really roar the words out and wave his arms about happily. Strangely, most of the locals he knew seemed a bit reserved, even puzzled. One night we were drinking with some artists, and Scott went off to the toilet. One of them said something that reduced the others to hysterics. I asked our guide what he'd said.

'He said that Scott speaks Romanian like a handicapped man from Hungary ... who has not visited Romania for some time.'

Scott had a habit of wandering about the flat naked. He is a big man and has a body sort of like an enormous turtle. I would lie in bed hungover of a morning, hoping that he'd put on some clothes before I got up. He's an impatient chap and he'd march up and down frustratedly outside my room, eager to set off on the day's trip to some deserted shipbuilding town. The local all-meat diet took its toll and one day I was unable to get up so just lay in bed farting, loud ones that sounded like a round of applause in hell. I could see the big, pink shadow of Scott pacing angrily just beyond the dimpled glass of the door. He burst into my room, actually burst in naked, to a room so filled with eldritch fumes that he was hit with a sort of backdraught. Straining to sit up, I could see his huge naked form kneeling in the hallway, retching onto the floor like a dying animal.

At the very end of the trip we went to a Romanian wedding. I challenged everybody at the wedding to a drinking competition. Obviously everybody had a lifetime's experience of drinking the local moonshines and prison-liquors, so it wasn't going to be easy. Still, nobody had approached drinking with quite my level of single-minded dedication so it ended up being between me and a grumpy, alcoholic artist. I remember his last words being 'Let's call this a draw', as he lapsed into unconsciousness and slid off his chair onto the floor. This was the very last drinking I did and I certainly bowed out in style. It just seemed like a good note to go out on. Also, I suddenly saw very clearly that it would ruin my life and kill me.

Fresh off the booze, I decided to take up taekwondo, which I loved but was pretty terrible at. There was a really great school in Glasgow run by a proper Korean grandmaster and I'd do that two or three days a week. I even went on a week's training camp at one point. The whole thing is built on 'Indomitable Spirit', an ability to never give in. During camp I found that I had a 'Defatigible Spirit' and gave in. I really miss it, actually. My next tour is going to be the last one and hopefully I can get into a martial art after it's all over. There's just no way that being able to do a rowdy gig in Hull makes you cooler than somebody who can punch their way through a wall.

*   *   *

Apart from the taekwondo I was spending a lot of my social time at the Stand. One of the bar staff was a guy in his late twenties called Rob. He was a nice man, with a tremendous and undermining hunger for drugs and sex that he was always trying to keep a lid on. He was like a cartoon – you could see all the vices he held at bay written in strained lines across his face. He was just desperately trying to keep a grip. I knew him as this very quiet, sincere guy but occasionally you heard stories of the door to his personal dungeon blowing open and the craziness he'd get up to. One night I stayed at his flat after a show and in the morning we got a cab back to the club. The taxi driver was giving off this really weird vibe, silently watching us in the mirror for the whole journey then taking his fare without a word.

'Wonder what's up with that guy,' I laughed.

Rob revealed that he may have phoned the cab company the week before while high. Someone who may well have been that driver had arrived to find Rob with his shirt off dancing in his driveway to pounding techno shouting, 'Have you got any drugs?' For future reference, it would seem that cabbies hate that.

I went on the Stand's inaugural Highland Tour. There were five of us in Tommy's Mercedes doing gigs in towns with names so Scottish they sounded like they'd been made up for a Disney musical. Jane was compering on the tour and was particularly challenging. Very funny doing the shows, not so funny treating us all to a synaptic meltdown as Tommy drove at 100 mph along country roads. I decided to poison her. I got a whole load of powerful diarrhoea drugs and was going to spike her drink until one of the other acts talked me out of it. He made a convincing case that there was a fair chance that diarrhoea wouldn't make her quit the tour and we just tried to tune out the madness for another week.

The Stand was also running workshops for beginner comedians and I would teach at some of them. The students formed a bewildering and exhaustive wall chart of the nuances of mental illness. One early class involved a big guy who had jokes that sort of went:

'I was fucking this coon ... It was a racooon! ... I was fucking this black bird ... feathers everywhere!'

I said I didn't think that on a Saturday night the use of the word 'coon' was going to go down particularly well. One of the other guys at the back threw his hands up in exasperation and said, 'Isn't this just political correctness gone mad?!'

Later at the bar I suggested he say, 'I was fucking a pair of blue tits. I'm a necrophiliac!' and he told me he found that utterly offensive.

There was a little bloke there who, how can I put this, didn't have Down's syndrome but looked like he did. Nothing was actually wrong with him, but something clearly wasn't right. He had two different acts, one as himself and one as a female poet. Every show, he'd agonise endlessly about which of these terrible, mirthless acts to perform. When he'd dress up as a woman there was a genuine thrill of Victorian circus horror that would run through the crowd – somebody once described it as looking like the scene where ET staggers out of the cupboard. Once I was compering a new-act night in Edinburgh and he was asking me whether I thought he should do his character that night. I grumpily told him to just do it as himself and he blurted, 'But I wore these all the way here!' and turned round to reveal that he had an enormous pair of fake boobs under his jumper. He'd sat on the train from Glasgow – looking at his best he'd have drawn a freak-show crowd in Middle Earth – wearing these huge pointy knockers.

There was another guy called 'Mudfinger'. He was quite a bammy Glasgow guy who had hit on the idea of playing a Tolkienesque character who could turn things to mud with his magical finger. He'd come on stage wearing a bed-sheet toga and his magical finger was an empty toilet-roll tube he'd taped to his hand. He'd do a bit of a preamble, explaining his power and then, fair fucks to the guy, would genuinely start trying to turn stuff into mud. That's where it could start to go a bit awry, because he never did get the hang of actually turning things into mud, but you've got to love a tryer haven't you? The audiences thought not and nearly killed him on a few occasions.

I got genuinely depressed by the workshops in the end. The sheer unrelenting needy madness of the fuckers was too much for me, and I'd worked in an asylum. The last one I did was with the comedian Susan Morrison. While they went through their acts on the stage I found a Valium someone had given me on a night out once that I'd always kept in my wallet for emergencies. I swallowed it surreptitiously and lay down behind the bar, praying that Susan would be able to think of something positive for me to say to them.

There's a real link between comedy and mental illness, I think largely because travelling and doing gigs is fucking exhausting. Put Richard Dawkins on a train to gig round the north of England and in ten days he'll be throwing shit at the walls. Speaking of being mental, there's no easy way to break this to you. I saw a UFO. Two of them actually, hovering above Charing Cross in Glasgow. Now what the fuck would aliens be doing there? It's the sort of place you only stop at if it's on the way somewhere; you'd never actually go there deliberately. It just seems really weird that aliens would travel millions of miles and manifest there, rather than say the West End or Merchant City. I was stepping out of a café and a big thing that looked like three interconnected silver balls stopped and hovered maybe 500 feet up in the air. Another thing that was exactly the same joined it, they both sat there completely still for a bit, then shot off together at a really ridiculous speed. I ran in that general direction for a bit, hoping I'd get another look. In Glasgow a running man, looking desperately up into the sky, doesn't attract any attention at all.

I don't really believe in aliens as such. I suppose I feel that alien life would be genuinely alien, not ships or humanoids or whatever. Terence McKenna has an essay about how magic mushrooms might be alien, that a different kind of thought is as close as we'll get to an alien experience. That's what I think an alien contact would be like, an unforeseeable event that would leave us with a new number between one and ten or a single word that described the feeling when you got a really bad DVD and it wasn't quite shit enough to be funny.

However, I do believe that the government has a lot of military hardware it develops and doesn't tell us about. That's what I reckon these things were, unmanned drone technology. I told everybody when this happened and they all put it down to me having drunk a whole cafetière of coffee just before I saw them. Trust me, as a comedy writer I have drunk as much coffee as anybody in the world. If that stuff made you hallucinate UFOs my life would have been a lot more fucking interesting. But I do have it on good authority that our governments made contact with aliens years ago. They came here looking for water for their dying planet. Now all they want is cocaine.

Why is it that even though there are now great cameras on mobile phones, every UFO picture is still a blurry shot of what looks like a Fray Bentos pie tin being thrown over a hedge? Bonnybridge in Scotland is one of the top places for sightings. Then again, in Bonnybridge you're an alien if you have ten fingers. Files were recently released that are being called Britain's X-Files. They're quite a bit shitter than the American X-Files though. They get abductions, cows missing organs and the alien probes up their bottoms. What have we got in our X-Files? An out-of-focus picture of a kite and an eyewitness account from a drunk man of mysterious lights appearing in the sky over Gatwick. I mean, why do aliens always abduct rural alcoholics? If we travelled for the thousands of years it would take to find intelligent life, I doubt we'd say, 'Let's go over and talk to that guy, the one who's crapping into his own hand. He must be some sort of ambassador.'

I'm sure it was totally unrelated to my UFO sighting but I was smoking a fair bit of dope then, mostly as a sort of mind salt that made bad television palatable. Eventually you realise that you are pretty much constructing your own shows, bathed in a flickering ultraviolet banality while writing parallel telly in your head. Most of the telly was rubbish and I needed the dope to liven it up. But I did make a few good discoveries. One of my all-time heroes is now a guy called Tom Weir. He was a Scottish walker and climber who did a show called *Weir's Way* in the early Eighties. It has an ethereal quality, like it could have been made a hundred years ago. Or perhaps it's that Scotland in 1982 was quite like the nineteenth century. He simply asked people about stuff that nobody else would ask. I remember a show where he asked an old miner what he used to get in his pieces, and there was a fantastic one where he went to a Scottish village where Lawrence of Arabia spent some time after a nervous breakdown. Little is known of Lawrence's time there, but Tom managed to track down a man who, as a wee boy, had run errands for him.

'So what can you tell us about T. E. Lawrence?'

'Well, Tom, he loved a Mint Imperial!'

There's another great episode where he visited a school on an island and talked to this frightening-looking headmistress with thick glasses, who had modelled her hairstyle on Einstein. He spoke to her about the difficulties of schooling children on an island and she talked proudly of the new school computer. Cut to a loving shot of an old BBC Acorn computer in a shed somewhere, a shot that goes on for ages. Tom seemed enthused and asked if the kids could use the computer whenever they liked.

'Oh, no', she replied, shocked. 'We can't be sending Mr McKenzie down to switch on the generator every day!'

I also started doing Mexican magic mushrooms with Paul Marsh. They used to be available legally from headshops and are a tremendous thing – they give you a real feeling of poetic clarity. Once I saw the comic-book hero Iron Man appear silhouetted on my bedroom wall. I knew that if I took more mushrooms, Iron Man would walk out of the wall and start speaking to me, so I went to bed. A missed opportunity. Another time I became obsessed with the idea that the mushrooms had let me see an important truth that explained everything and desperately looked for pen and paper to write it down. When I got up in the morning I discovered that in the centre of a sheet of A4 I had written in tiny letters, 'Language is meaningless.'

*   *   *

I started compering the Stand's Thursday nights every week. I did Glasgow for a bit and later did a couple of years of the same thing in Edinburgh. It was interesting to do the same local gig so often. After a while, I could walk through town on my way there and sense how many people would be at the show and what the atmosphere would be like.

As with anything you overdo, a lot of weird stuff started to happen. I remember doing the Thursday that was the first ever night of the Glasgow Comedy Festival. A woman went nuts screaming that she was on anti-depressants and they were bombing Baghdad. I'm still not sure how the two were linked, but some audience members took it upon themselves to pick her up and run out through the fire doors with her, using her as a kind of battering ram. Encouraged by this, the next week when I had another nutter throw her drink at me, I just asked a really big punter to pick her up and run away. He did, and neither of them ever came back. They both left their coats. He might have killed her for all I know. I hope he has.

That said, any function has the potential to be pretty weird. I know a comic who had to do a student ball somewhere. It was fancy dress and the only person who came into the bit where he was performing was a student dressed as a jester, with a bell on the end of his hat. The organisers still insisted the comic did his full show.

'40 minutes I did,' he told me, 'and that fucking bell didn't ring once.'

Once I performed at some kind of student ball at Cambridge at about two in the morning. I find it difficult to be on stage at a time when I'm normally a couple of hours into a sexually charged nightmare. To worsen the matter, I drank one of those brutal energy drinks. This one might as well have had the slogan 'A 36-hour erection in a can'. There was a fair bit of heckling, which I could only deal with by threatening to come off stage and kill people. This went down pretty well, I think because people thought I was some sort of ironic Scottish character act, rather than genuinely suppressing a murderous, sleep-deprived rage. As I left, a hypnotist was taking the stage. How hard can it be to hypnotise a bunch of drunken students at two in the morning? I can only hope he led them all off like the Pied Piper and drowned them in the river.

The next night I was in Scotland to perform in a castle for an association of small-shop owners ('No Muslim jokes please, Frankie'). It was a lot more fun with pipers, me and then a display of falconry. There's nothing like waiting to go on stage and being told to keep it tight because it's 'past the eagle's bedtime'.

I kept doing the Edinburgh show for way too long because one of the barmaids was really attractive. In fact, there aren't words to describe it. She was really attractive in the way that the Taj Mahal is really attractive. I've always been attracted to women who are out of my league and it's gotten easier to find them as I've got older and uglier. It wasn't a lust thing, more an admiration of beauty; everybody has a view they love and that was the view I loved. I'd pretend to be looking out at the audience pre-show and would actually just watch her, boredly washing tumblers. The other comedians all thought I was obsessed with what our audience looked like. She hated comedy, making her perfect. I didn't really ever get to know her properly. It probably would have spoiled it all.

Eventually she left and I packed it in too. I'd always go out on a Thursday night, cycling round Pollok Estate then sitting and having a joint under a tree where you'd often see a lot of wee birds, squirrels and the like. At first I thought I was cycling to use up the adrenaline I'd have when I'd normally be doing a show. Eventually I realised I was just trying to replace the beauty in my life. I've debated whether or not this whole section is a good thing to admit to. I think Britain is probably too uptight to enjoy such a story. If the book gets translated into French, this bit will win me some kind of award.

Incidentally, while on the subject of romance, here is what I have learned from my adventures of the heart. Drugs are better than Love. If there was a drug that had a comedown like Love, you would never take it. Here, pssst, take this. You'll feel fantastic for a while, then after the high has gone you'll feel like someone has plunged a broken shard of window pane repeatedly through your chest while reciting all your failings in a flat monotone. You'll feel like that every day for about four years. Take it! I'm kidding; if you see a chance for love, go for it. Throw everything you've got at it like you're a fool. Life without love is a fucking wilderness. It's only the invention of MDMA that has stopped me throwing myself under a bus. I

really don't have the words for how I'd like to end this chapter, so I'd like you to imagine the long howl of an animal in
pain.

TWELVE

For a wee while I was quite happy travelling around doing clubs but the stag parties, the Proclaimers-based heckles and the guys who'd storm it after me doing comedy songs about Viagra started to take their toll. I wanted to do something a bit different and my real break into telly was a show I did in Scotland called *Live Floor Show*. Comics often wonder about whether they network enough, or have the right agent to get a break. I literally just got an email from a producer who had never met me that said, 'Hello from the BBC', and suddenly I was on TV.

It was a stand-up show hosted by Greg Hemphill, who is hugely famous in Scotland from *Chewing the Fat* and *Still Game*. There was also a camp, gay chap called Craig Hill, who had a lovely voice like a sort of velvety suggestion. Jim Muir was the Reverend Obadiah Steppenwolfe III, a drug-loving sex-hungry sociopath whom we quickly discovered to be a toned-down version of Jim's real personality. Miles Jupp played an aristocratic English lord, indulging in the brutal Scot-baiting that we all enjoyed but without the safety net. Paul Sneddon had a football character called Bob Doolally and did brilliant sketches that were like little three-panel comic strips in a newspaper, perhaps one that had a pretty broadminded approach to obscenity.

We filmed the credits for the show in a lap-dancing bar and they'd hired one of the regular dancers to show us how to pole dance. Looking back, it was an insight into what the producers really thought of us. I often play a game in the street where I look for a face that would make me leave a house party. Someone so debased or villainous looking that the minute they walked in I'd have to go before the whole thing descended into heroin and handcuffs. This bitch would have had me cracking the bathroom window open and scuttling down the drainpipe. She demonstrated a variety of basic moves we could try, while her 9-year-old daughter watched judgementally from a barstool. She told me that she did private dances but the one rule was that her knickers stayed on. 'Doesn'y mean you canny hitch 'em to the side', she added, with a conspiratorial grunt that stopped me fucking my girlfriend for about a fortnight.

The actual credits they used on the show featured me doing the splits at the base of the pole, always a good way to introduce topical comedy. Paul Sneddon went to lick the pole during his bit and we all virtually bundled him to the ground. It was a moment of madness on his part – think of all the desperate vaginas that had gripped that metal. He might as well have sucked Gene Simmons's cock.

Working in mental health made me ideally qualified for doing a programme with BBC Scotland. We were an in-house production, which meant I got to deal with people who were lazy, moody or daft to the point where it could have been registered as a handicap. The whole department appeared to make about two or three shows a year, a workload everybody seemed to find absolutely harrowing. You'd go into the office and they'd all just be sitting playing internet poker. Later, when I first started working in London, I was really struck by how messy the offices were – scripts and DVDs piled on desks and researchers running around. It seemed chaotic and unnatural to see people actually working.

Naturally, both the producers on the show were English. One was just some kind of figurehead; he'd come down and drink wine in the green room before a recording and tell hugely implausible stories about celebrities he knew. Who knows, maybe he thought he was fulfilling some kind of function there, like perhaps we needed settling before a performance, and the only way to achieve this was by listening to a long-winded story about a 1970s children's TV presenter who had a specially adapted ambulance that he used to sexually abuse the disabled.

Our main producer was a plausible, bulshitty media type. We'd go off and write the show every week, and his job was to edit it so that just before a punchline there would be a sudden cutaway to a shot taken from fifty feet up in the air, or of some people talking in the crowd. Rising to the top in BBC Scotland must be a lot like getting ahead in the Bolivian air force – nobody has much idea of what's going on, so the bluffers will thrive. Most of the senior people there would, in another walk of life, have had a job like Pizza Hut franchise manager. Although probably not for long.

The producers of *LFS* would come to the try-out show we did every week and sit in the crowd, putting little ticks or crosses against our jokes. They'd veto stuff for quite random reasons ('Don't do a joke about him, my wife's reading his autobiography'), and we'd sometimes have to go away afterwards and write new stuff through the night. It was a bit of a grind some weeks, but it meant I became really prolific at writing new stuff. Also – I'm going to say this because sometimes I need reminding – sitting up stoned thinking of jokes and watching MTV Base isn't a very hard job.

It was during that period that I started smoking dope to write. It really helped me to think sideways. I can't ever remember sitting down with a load of grass and worrying that I wasn't going to get the job done. All the jokes that got blocked meant I'd have to write maybe ten minutes of short, topical gags a week. That's a lot more than is practical and I needed the drugs to do it. Even Jay Leno with the best writers in America is only doing five or six minutes. If you ever see Jay Leno opening with a tight ten, you can be pretty sure that he's stoned out of his mind. That's why I've always thought it must be great being George Michael. Getting stoned and waiting for that wave to wash over you. That wave of realisation ... 'I'm George Michael!' OK, it's naughty for him to drive under the influence but in his defence, he is going really, really slowly.

I've not smoked for years, but I was pretty horrified when cannabis was reclassified from Class C to Class B. That's only going to confuse people, especially cannabis users. Somehow, I can't imagine the whole reclassification has hit the cannabis industry very hard.

'Let's go out and get stoned and have a good time!'

'I take it you haven't seen today's *Guardian* then? No more cannabis for us, we're going to need to find some really time-consuming hobbies. That make bad television seem amusing.'

We were pretty unusual for a TV programme in that we'd all go and party after the show. They'd pay for hotel rooms in Glasgow and we'd all go back and get hammered. Everybody else drank but myself and Jim would drop pills and get stoned. I can't really imagine that happening on *Mock the Week*, but it would be great if it had. I sincerely regret never having had a night where Rory Bremner, Hugh Dennis and I got high on MDMA powder while vibing to the latest hip-hop videos. There's still time.

I remember one day the production crew gave us a row about a drugs reference in one of the warm-up shows. I can't remember the joke, but it was just Jim saying that I was skinning up for him backstage, which I was. They thought it was a bad thing to associate the show with. That night after filming they came to our hotel and got steaming. They all had a massive argument with the staff as they tried to get up to our rooms to continue the party. We were in my room and could hear them being chased along the corridors by security guards, screaming. Next day, I saw all the production notes from the show strewn on the steps, together with scripts and the acts' phone numbers. Overall, that show's production was the most chaotic, wrongheaded thing I've ever seen in any field of human endeavour. The whole experience was like being in a farcical movie about comedians dealing with a group of inept bank robbers who had taken over a TV production and for some reason had to make a show before they could escape with their bank-robbery money.

Miles Jupp's monologues as a pompous old monied lord were hilarious in their vicious snobbery and deliberate anti-Scottishness. It was the first time I understood comedy as a sublimation of our real personalities. Miles was, as a person, somewhat horrified and disgusted by the world and his character was able to express that in a sort of cartoon form. While we were doing the second series Miles got a job as Archie the Inventor on *Balamory*. I used to try to keep him up getting pissed when he had to film in the morning, just so that years later I'd have the pleasure of switching on CBeebies and seeing a man staggering around like a zombie in a kilt, trying to make a telephone from yoghurt tubs. For one extraordinary moment I almost presented a kids' TV show. It was a thing where I lived in a house somewhere with a bunch of wee puppets that would make little arts-and-crafts-type things and show them to me, their human pal. I met the producers and said that I wanted to play it as if my character was a schizophrenic. I'd be seen doing push-ups at the start of every episode, and would share my house with a normal family downstairs. Occasionally you'd see them talking to me, and my puppets would be lifeless, as if the whole thing was part of my paranoid imagination. Bizarrely, they were quite up for that and arranged for me to come do a screen test. Clearly I would have ended up being like Krusty the Klown if this had come off. I was supposed to rehearse a little song-and-dance number for the audition. I just couldn't do it. I phoned them up and felt odd to hear the words coming out of my mouth as I told them in a choked voice, 'I just can't sing the little song, I just can't do the little dance.'

For a while, Paul Sneddon drifted into doing the sort of gigs that Bob Doolally would have had. He did a lot of sporting dinners and terrifying sounding corporate functions. He told me about one where he turned up early and asked if there was a dressing room.

'A dressing room?' said the man who'd let him in, pronouncing each word like it was completely new to him.

'Yes, so I can put on my wig … for the character.'

'You're wearing a wig?' The guy was in deep shock. 'You're a poofy bastard!'

I was killing myself laughing when Paul told me this, but there was more.

'Thing is,' Paul told me, 'this guy was doing the vote of thanks at the end!'

Apparently the guy stood up after dinner and thanked everybody involved. When he got to Paul he said,

'Thanks to Bob Doolally … for being shite.'

I also did Scottish corporate shows, and at one the organiser came up to me before I went on and said the one thing that would really make you wonder why he'd hired a comedian. 'Remember son, no smart remarks!' Incredible. Nowadays a Scottish corporate gig means telling gags to queues outside soup kitchens. They can be tough gigs – a Scottish businessman's idea of humour is farting on a golf course. To be fair, when your life consists of selling automated garage doors the last thing you want is a sense of irony. I know they say you should tailor your gigs to the audience but I refuse to wear flares and tell jokes about Ugandans. The advantage of these gigs is how healthy they make me feel. The only time you'll see more fat guys in suits is at a darts player's funeral. It's like looking at an M&S window display reflected in the back of a teaspoon.

I'm one of the few Scottish comedians who never get booked to do a Burns supper, having done one where some business arse offered me his performance advice afterwards and I offered to punch him in the mouth. Actually, I'd done one before that, at some old military club in London. In the event of an invasion this base will be a real asset. If it took me and the taxi driver an hour to find it with a satnav, the Chinese have got no chance. I went into the room and it was a beautiful ballroom. It looked like a movie set. There was a piper playing and he looked immaculate, like one of those old lead army figures come to life.

'I'm the comedian!' I told the organiser.

'No, we have Richard Wilson,' he hissed back.

I played upstairs standing on an improvised stage that was an empty ammo box, while the organiser held an anglepoise lamp over my head so people could see me. I did a wee question-and-answer session at the end.

'Who do you hate most in showbusiness?' someone piped up.

'Fucking Richard Wilson!' I growled, to everybody's bemusement.

That said, it's no surprise that people sometimes choose to hire me to host a corporate awards ceremony. I'm an asset at such events with my stony face and lack of interpersonal skills. Also, I have such a huge lack of understanding of business; the people I meet might as well be telling me that they're fairies for all I understand of what they do. Anyway, one time a prize winner was having her photo taken with me and tried to shove her finger up my arse. I suppose that doing a corporate show,

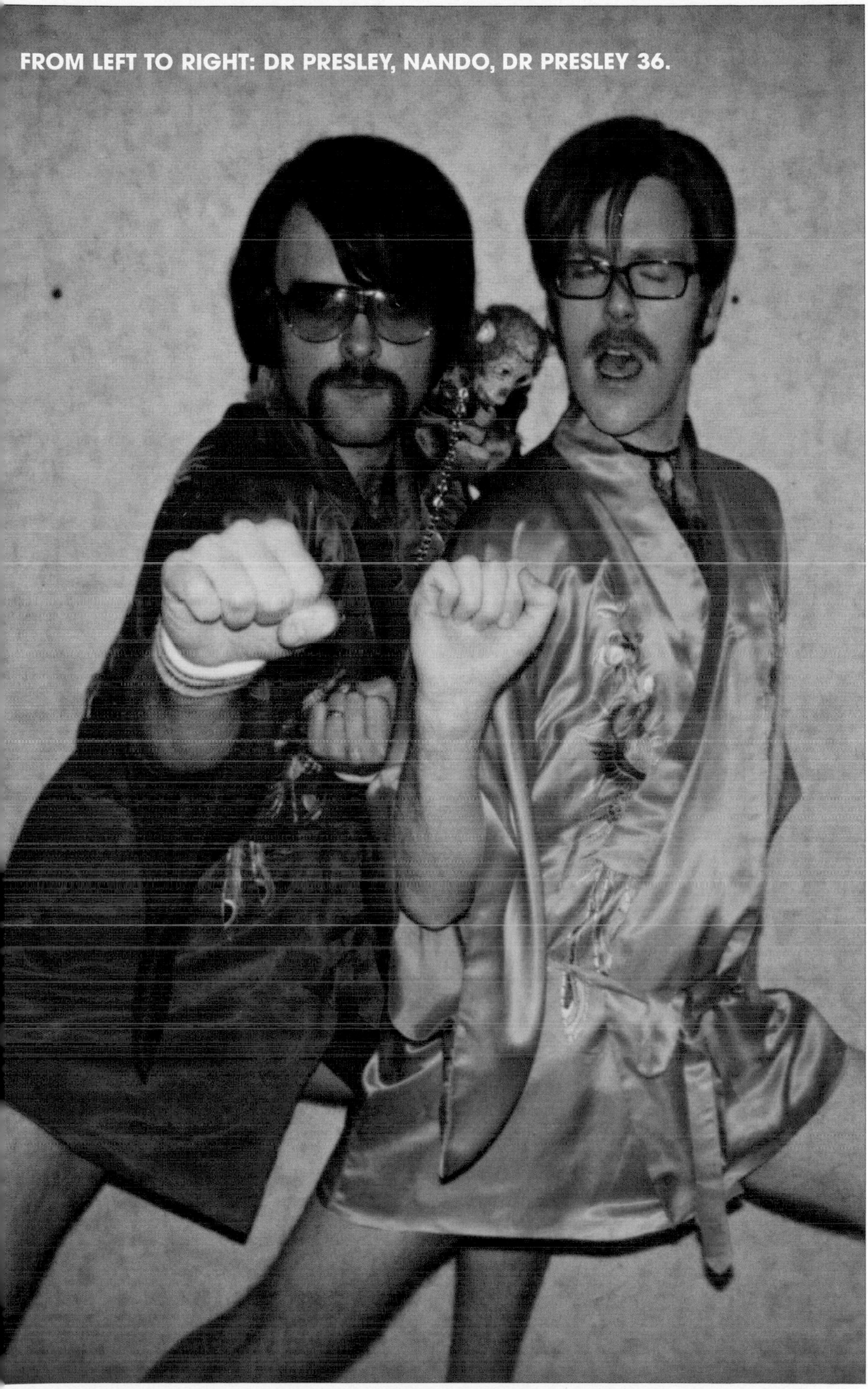

FROM LEFT TO RIGHT: DR PRESLEY, NANDO, DR PRESLEY 36.

I KEPT THIS LOOK FOR YEARS.

SEVILLE. I FEEL, AND LOOK, COOL.

TAKEN FROM INSIDE MY DREAMS.

LOCH LOMOND WITH MY DAUGHTER.

BEING A DAD ISN'T TIRING. IF ANYTHING, IT GIVES YOU MORE ENERGY.

THE ONE RECORDED INSTANCE OF PAUL MARSH REGISTERING ON NORMAL FILM.

JIM AND I HATING THE EDINBURGH FESTIVAL.

FRANK SKINNER IMAGINES EVERYBODY WILL BE PROFESSIONAL AND SMILE. HATS OFF TO HIM. THE NEXT WEEK WE WERE BOTH ON *YOU HAVE BEEN WATCHING* AND HE SAID SOMETHING THAT MADE ME LAUGH FOR A WEEK AND A HALF.

MOCKING THAT FUCKING WEEK.

I THINK THE KEY TO COMEDY IS TO LOOK LIKE YOU'RE TRYING TO INTERNALISE A BEREAVEMENT.

GOOD OLD HUGH. THE ENGLISH CUNT.

I THEN PRODUCED THE
FLAGS OF ALL NATIONS.

that's kind of where you're taking it anyway. God, I really wish I had that photo.

Something fairly bizarre happens at almost every one of those shows. The other night the guy who was introducing me got in a quick plea for money for his polio charity. I don't know if there's such a thing as an ideal introduction, but this one started with 'Ladies and Gentlemen, I want you to cast your mind back to 1950 when polio was the AIDS of its day.' Some of these shows are alright, but round about Christmas they all get like those parties Fred Flintstone and Barney used to show up at in their water-buffalo hats.

The whole idea of corporate sponsorship in itself is pretty weird. I love the fact Stella Artois sponsor Film 4, 'cos boy does Stella make you think of arthouse films. I'd like to think how some films would pan out if you added Stella. I'd like to see *Brief Encounter* where Celia Johnson and Trevor Howard agonise about forbidden love. Add a couple of Stellas and he's nuts deep in her in the station toilet, she's combing the sick out of her hair. *Kramer vs. Kramer* – a great analysis of a man coming to love his son before a heart-wrenching courtroom scene where he battles for custody with his ex-wife. Add a couple of Stellas – he turns up for court wearing just a towel and an electronic parrot he's programmed to tell the judge to go fuck himself.

For the second *Live Floor Show* series on BBC Scotland I started writing for Craig Hill. That was great fun and lasted for a few years; we wrote a load of his telly performances and a couple of his Fringe shows together. I'd toodle round to his flat for about ten in the morning, and then we'd gossip about celebrities for half an hour and eat doughnuts and drink coffee. I was surprised at how big a gay side I had to draw on. He's a gloriously witty man and he'd make me laugh every day. Craig said he'd sit and watch his shows with his friends and they'd be shocked that the campest stuff had generally been written by me. I've always had a slightly snobbish, judgemental side, so I could write catty. Not that any of it would have worked if it wasn't channelled through Craig's enthusiasm and showmanship. Craig liked to do audience putdowns, so it was fun writing cruel lines for his adoring crowds.

'Hello, madam! I've always loved people who have the ability to do make-up in the car. Did you hit a couple of speed-bumps?'

That kind of thing. My particular favourite, which he could sell with just the right jolly callousness was:

'Don't worry, madam. One day you'll meet a man who'll love you for what you are. Forty.'

I often wondered how the world's very first gay guy got on in caveman society.

'I made a pass at Steve the other day – he wasn't into it but luckily I managed to pass it off as a wrestling hold. I wish somebody would hurry up and invent beer.'

It was during the second series of that show that I really got into doing topical, political stuff as it was interesting being on TV at a time of various political fuck-ups. The massive overspend on the Scottish parliament building, for example, basically confirmed the image we'd all had of Scottish politicians being corrupt or incompetent. After all, the whole idea of politicians commissioning buildings and redesigning town centres is ridiculous. Having spent a lifetime blinking through senseless meetings about towpaths, they are the most tasteless people on earth. Would you let an MSP decorate your front room? Politicians simply can't be trusted to spend public money on anything stylish. And yet no reply to my proposal to the parliament that every candidate should be forced to have a running mate who is a flamboyant homosexual.

Do you know what occurs to me from a few years of writing gags about the various scandals and fuck-ups? It seems that our politicians aren't very good at organising things. Now some of us would have thought that being organised would be exactly the sort of thing a politician should be good at. That is simply naïve. Just as you or I forget to pay a bill or are late with a tax return, a politician will consider it a good week if he has not released hundreds of rapists onto the streets or accidentally closed down a world-class medical facility. One of the great things about politicians is that they sit in their highly paid jobs always teetering on the edge of disaster. Never knowing which of their recent decisions – based entirely on ill-informed guesswork – might be about to dash their career to pieces.

Take the Iraq war, for example. The news at the time was dominated by the war and the government was being criticised for not giving soldiers more medals. To be fair it was really difficult finding enough bits left to pin them on. British forces have helped train 20,000 Iraqi troops; hopefully not too well though, as we'll be going back to fight them in ten years' time. According to the UN our presence in Iraq in 2009 is totally illegal, even if we are only there as a training force. The excuse 'It's not illegal, I'm only here teaching them English' didn't work for Gary Glitter, nor should it work for the military.

If there is a lesson to be learned from Iraq, it must be this. Never invade a country where everyone has guns. These are people who take six guns to a barbeque. Iraqi *Antiques Roadshow* is probably an endless parade of 1970s rocket-propelled grenade launchers. 'No, I'm not going to get it insured, Hugh. I'm going to fire it into a queue outside a police station.'

I also started writing for Jim doing the Reverend Obadiah Steppenwolfe III. We would get really stoned and take ecstasy and write from noon till about ten at night. One particularly drug-fuelled writing day led to a truly mental sketch where the Reverend presided over a wedding between a member of the audience and a sinister character we'd invented called Chauncey O'Hallorahan Junior. Chauncey was a military fantasist played by the comedian Sandy Nelson and had lines that I could barely tell anyone for laughing, delivered in a droll American monotone.

'I get all the vitamins I need eating pussy. And vitamin supplements.'

'I once made love to a bride on her wedding day. Felt like I came in the cake.'

And my favourite, the inexplicable greeting he gives to the 'bride' who gets dragged from the audience:

'When I ride you, I will be resplendent like a Griffin.'

One night during the series, I went to lend moral support to Jim when he did a charity gig with Phil Kay. Moral support in this context means 'roll joints'. They were doing a show for a homeless charity and it was packed out. The organiser was a bubbly little Australian who'd only just started in her job and this was the first event she'd put on. There was a lot of beer about and we managed to get her quite drunk and stoned. Phil was going through a phase where he just sang his whole act, accompanying himself on a guitar, despite not really being able to play. He did the first half by himself – it was great too, he's still the only comedian who is genuinely just making it all up.

'Is Jim going to sing too?' asked the organiser. 'I really think the crowd would like him to sing.'

I came back with 'I think the crowd would like to hear you sing!' – a proposition which she took strangely seriously. Seeing the possibility for chaos, I pressed her on it, insisting that the evening would be strangely lacking if she didn't go on and belt out a few crowd pleasers. Jim did his show and then, as we were sitting backstage smoking, it became apparent that the lady had taken to the stage with Phil and begun a long, improvised song. We looked through the curtain to see them both sat at the edge of the stage, swaying gently as she sang about what would appear to have been quite a lonely childhood. Her boss came backstage afterwards looking shell-shocked.

'That was great, wasn't it?' we suggested, as he struggled to chew down a mixture of anger and confusion.

'Well,' he eventually offered, 'I think we should have maybe had the raffle during the interval, instead of at the end.'

Brilliant. That was clearly what had gone wrong with the evening, we all agreed.

THIRTEEN

At the same time as appearing on the *Live Floor Show*, I got a job writing for another TV programme in Scotland, a hugely misguided panel show called *Caledonia McBrains*. It was supposed to be like a Scottish version of *Have I Got News For You*, but the BBC wanted to use archive rather than current news footage. We'd kick off every week by making the panel do gags about the local news from 1973. It was truly an amazing disaster but got quite a bit of coverage, for example two pages of the *Daily Record* under the headline 'The Worst Show Ever'. It was a fun job though. Every week I'd pour all my efforts into filling the script with references to classical monsters. Minotaurs, Mermen, Griffins, on a good week it was like watching Dominik Diamond read aloud from a medieval bestiary. It also meant that I'd made the move to working full time in television, which made me wonder if I might be becoming a bit of a cunt.

I've always had a pretty ambivalent attitude to being on TV. It is, after all, just a shiny bauble used to distract morons while they're having their pockets picked. I don't actually own a telly – haven't for maybe seven or eight years. I found it to be brutally addictive and also just a drug I'd take without making a choice. If you want to get stoned you have to admit you want to get stoned and go find some drugs. If you want to experience the numbed high of watching two celebrities compete to see who can become the best plumber, you just drift into that hell without making a conscious decision.

A lot of people get quite conscious of their appearance because they're on TV. I can barely even be bothered to wash my face. Natalie Cassidy has revealed she is still unhappy when she looks in a mirror despite losing four stone and having a boob job. Could it be that her mirror is still showing her her face? She said that whenever she went out to dinner she would take a bag of laxatives with her. The laxatives to help clear the food, the bag to slip over her head should she spot a bloke she fancied.

Most television programmes underestimate our intelligence. I'd imagine that there are actually many animals in houses across Britain that are bored by *Dancing on Ice*. The fact that such a spectacle gets respectable viewing figures means that people take a lot more hardcore drugs than official statistics suggest. Only someone semi-conscious on a methadone and ketamine cocktail could actually enjoy seeing Ulrika Jonsson skate into some advertising hoardings. Or perhaps they're just too blasted to work the remote. And remember that stramash about the BBC proving itself to be unreliable? They showed footage that seemed to show the Queen storming out of a photo shoot in a huff. It transpired that she had actually stormed into the photo shoot in a huff and then had an argument.

The problem is that a lot of programming is just not quite appalling enough to be entertaining. *Children in Need* is the worst offender. Pudsey bear actually has two perfectly good eyes.

Inside his eyepatch he keeps a photo of a little crippled boy and he looks at it all through the show and pisses himself laughing. And what is *Comic Relief* really achieving? Fattening some little fucker up enough that he can get eaten by a crocodile? People in Africa aren't starving. They're fine. The whole thing got sorted out years ago when Jamie Oliver came up with a cheap and nutritious recipe for flies. In fact, the only people that live in Africa are Billy Connolly, Lenny Henry and Westlife. They've turned the whole of Africa into a big waterslide park using our money. Do you know what they do once a year? They get all the blankets and toys and stuff that we've sent in and they have a huge bonfire!

'That's it Lenny! Throw another incubator into the bonfire! That'd be brilliant! Some nutter sat in a bath full of beans for a week to buy that … ahhahaha! Oh this is brilliant!'

Hasn't Richard Curtis built up enough good karma over the years? He could stop *Comic Relief* now and still comfortably be in credit with the universe. In fact he could rape a special-needs basketball team. It would certainly be a lot more entertaining than watching French and Saunders parody *The Sixth Sense*. It's not that I'm totally against donating to *Comic Relief*. For example, I'll donate a million pounds if the whole cast touch the roof of their mouths with a loaded shotgun while riding on a rollercoaster. But people sitting in a bathful of beans for starving Africans? Send them the fucking beans!

Celebrities appear on these things to get exposure. Great, climb towards that money pot on the backs of dying children you sick, sick fucks. I'm appalled by telethons but I'd hate you to think that I don't do my bit. I give a lot of money to the Third World. Indirectly, through my investments in landmines and diamorphine. I've made more money out of Africa than Paul Simon.

There are a lot of shows out there that are boring or half-witted, but you feel that if they just lowered their standards a couple of notches it could all become genuinely fun. Here are a few examples of what I'd like to see.

THE 2050 HOUSE

A modern British family are set the task of living as they would in the year 2050. Dad doesn't go to work each day, he simply plugs a cable into his head and enters a virtual work world. This leaves him more time for his hobbies of tennis and golf, which he plays by plugging cables into his back and neck. Just as we feel we are getting to know the Jones family, they are all killed by the government for going outside without their Identity Hats.

CELEBRITIES ON ACID ON ICE

Just like *Dancing on Ice*, but with an opening sequence where Graham Norton hoses the celebrities down with liquid LSD. Imagine the entertainment to be had in seeing Emma Bunton skate erratically across screen believing she is being pursued by a fourth-dimensional entity. Then as she collapses to the ice, her face turns to camera and we see her howl her growing knowledge into a melting world.

CELEBRITY CELEBRITY BIG BROTHER

Instead of all the nobodies who do *Celebrity Big Brother*, we get some real celebrities. Clint Eastwood has a bitter argument with Bruce Willis over teabags. Will Smith becomes favourite as Madonna and Angelina Jolie fall out over who gets to adopt him. Tom Cruise is trodden on and later finished off by a cat.

COME ON OSAMA, PUT THE FUCKING WEST OUT OF ITS MISERY

A new show where foetuses are made to sing pop ballads as they compete for the right to exist. Each week a winner is chosen at random, while Patrick Kielty's grinning, idiotic face is projected onto the moon.

The success of programmes like *The Apprentice* and *Dragons' Den* has been painted by some as showing the public's interest in the world of business. Actually, we just like seeing idiots being told that they are idiots. I wouldn't be surprised to see someone on *Dragons' Den* with an FM radio that doubles up as a tampon (meaning that it only picks up Chris Moyles) or an all-in-one heroin users' kit that never sells because it keeps getting shoplifted.

My only brush with awards is that I was once at the Scottish BAFTAs. We were nominated for *Live Floor Show*. Just imagine the ordinary BAFTAs but with a room full of people you don't recognise. It's full of the most unglamorous-looking people you've ever seen. It's like they're filming a large bus stop with a free buffet. Jim had given an incredible series of performances and had been nominated as Best Newcomer. He was beaten by the guy off the Scott's Porridge Oats advert.

The actual BAFTAs might well have been created by our Lizard Masters to power some kind of Horror Battery at the centre of the earth. An annual event where we take the fakest people in our society and honour them with the award of a golden mask. Would we really be any poorer as a society if everyone in that room died? It would certainly make things more entertaining if they could work it into the ceremony. I'd enjoy watching Stephen Merchant trying to collect his award from a panther. The runners-up would be picked off by a chimp that's been taught to use a sniper rifle. Paul O'Grady would die without ever knowing that the headshot which killed him was a result not of hatred, but of the belief that it would earn his killer a piece of fruit.

It seems that performers nowadays appear on more awards shows than episodes of the thing that they're getting the awards for. Ricky Gervais has been given so many awards he keeps his house inside his trophy room. It would be good to at least see performers make honest acceptance speeches: 'I'd like to thank my mother for her coldness and making me compete for her love.'

Can you imagine if the rest of society was wiped out and just the people at the BAFTAs survived? There's no way they could form even a rudimentary society. The future of humanity would be to live as slaves of the insect world. Every year they would hold a ceremony to honour whoever had collected the most pollen.

Nobody was surprised by the recent voting scandals surrounding awards. At the last British Comedy Awards Robert Mugabe got best newcomer. The only difference between Mugabe and other comedians is that his syphilis has driven him insane.

And the Oscars go on for so long now that at the end they play a memorial show reel of everyone who died during the ceremony. The fact that people manage to stay awake at all is tribute to how, at that level of fame, the cocaine is amazing. If I won an Oscar I'd simply say, 'As an incredibly rich man I shall now read a list of people who can go screw themselves.' A lot of these celebrities cry when getting an Oscar. I think it's simply relief, just knowing their place on the Scientology space ark is secure.

Caledonia McBrains was swiftly cancelled and, during a break from working on *LFS*, Jim Muir and Sandy Nelson and I went to Rothesay to do a gig. It's a wee holiday town on the Isle of Bute, near Glasgow. There's a unique nostalgic, Victorian feel to the place, mixed with the kind of gentility and decrepitude that you find in any seaside town. We'd been hired by this little middle-aged English bloke called Malcolm, who looked and acted like a gay Dr Who. He and his wife had moved to Rothesay on the strength of a visit they'd made to the place on one of its rare sunny days. It had rained pretty solidly since and they were both clearly suffering and homesick. We knocked around town for the afternoon, then sat in a beer garden somewhere that had barbed wire along the walls.

I nodded at the barbed wire. 'You know what that means round a beer garden. People on this island steal patio furniture.'

'Aye,' said Sandy, 'and sell it to each other.'

Malcolm took us back to his place to party. I think that his wife wasn't too pleased because she locked herself in the living room and played *All by Myself* over and over again. We waved goodbye to her when we left, as she puffed a cigarette out of the window, mouthing along to the words in a way that made little smoke signals rise up into the night.

It was a good show, inside a theatre where big cottony drapes formed a kind of indoor tent. Afterwards Jim and I got stoned and came up with my favourite-ever idea. It was to be a double act called The Entertainments. They were two Victorian performers who travelled to other dimensions to perform shows. There they staged Harry Houdini-style tricks to disturbing audiences (we wrote one where they were aboard the Imperial Zeppelin of King Bohar the Bronze, another at the MOBO Awards). When a trick failed it could have tremendous consequences for that dimension; the colour blue might disappear or China might declare war on the sun. We wrote quite a bit of material and tried to get BBC Scotland to put it on the next series of *LFS* we were doing. They dismissed it as the ramblings of the deeply stoned. I honestly still don't know if it was idiocy or genius, so here is the script we wrote that night, perhaps inspired by the general weirdness of Rothesay, decide for yourself.

A guest introduces the item. This could be the singer from that week's band; Greg; the current Mr Scotland.

Guest: Ladies and Gentlemen. The Entertainments.

The phrase 'The Entertainments' is dubbed over with a scratchy vinyl recording of an otherworldly upper-class voice and the guest moves in a puppet-like way as they voice this, as if gripped by an unseen force.

Red velvet curtains open with a swish to reveal the set. The set is Barok the Living Stage: a dark mixture of reds and purples suggestive of a Victorian Music Hall. We see the pianist behind an 1980s Yamaha organ with Mr Salbutamon standing in readiness upstage. There is a large steam-powered clock standing on the stage and a large oval screen above and behind the performers.

The pianist plays Victorian-style organ music throughout the item, but breaks into snatches of inspiring Eighties power ballads while Mr Salbutamon is attempting his feats of amazement.

Pianist: It is our pleasure to be performing here tonight at the Lord Haringey School for the Rehabilitation and Violent Restraint of the Racially Ambiguous. Women and the uneducated may need to bite down on leather during the performance. Mr Salbutamon is here to amaze the mind and boggle the sensibilities. And of course fight the forces of entropy as they attempt to gnaw entry into our dimension.

Entropy sound effect on the organ 'ooh ahh ooh ahh' taken from the killer's intro music in Dirty Harry.

Pianist: I ... am here too! Mr Salbutamon has an exemplary record of achievement in the fields of Illusionism, Bind Breaking, Telepathy and Marksmanship. His insistence that he could only shoot on Whitsun and during a total eclipse meant that he did not receive the crimson ruby at this year's Berlin Olympics.

Unfortunately at a recent performance held at the King Albert Hall in New Berlin, Mr Salbutamon was defeated by Nektia the sub-demon of effeminacy in a high-stakes game of blindfold backgammon. Chance is a tempestuous whore! As a consequence ... this is now Lloyd Cole.

Splat. Jelly falls from ceiling and hits deck. Guy comes and scrapes him off floor with shovel and puts him a container on the organ. The pianist coughs awkwardly as he addresses the jelly.

Pianist: Lloyd. Tonight Barok the Living Stage is being powered by Indifference.

Shutter goes up to reveal a glass container in which there is a disco with a chap dancing round a dog. Barok grumbles. Gas comes up and fills the container.

Pianist: We found Barok the Living Stage wet and starving in a basement in the shantytowns of Outer Berlin. As we stood there we asked ourselves, 'Could this be living?' Tonight's first spectacle of wonder shall be the mordant carnival of sensory manipulation which Platinious called 'The Corruption of Possibility'.

Salbutamon brings out a fan of playing cards.

Pianist: Pick one! Ha! Success! The six of hearts. Ladies and gentlemen, you have just witnessed 'The Corruption of Possibility'.

While the pianist is announcing this, children with blank flour bags over their heads and feet – called Pheenome – roll out a step for Salbutamon to stand on and an ear trumpet that goes up to Salbutamon's arse.

Pianist: Compared with our next feat of amazement, even the mighty pyramids of Berlin are naught. Ladies and gentlemen, Mr Salbutmon gives you 'The Six Pillars of Zeus', where-in he shall manipulate his gastric tunnels to vocalise classic works of literature.

Salbutamon lets rip a huge fart which turns into a cough.

Pianist: Ah, a practice stroke. To prepare for this trial Mr Salbutamon has been drinking brandy and followed the *Boys Brigade Manual for Sudden Physical Exercise on Cold Mornings.*

Duality! Not only is Mr Salbutamon's reputation at stake. On the accomplishment of this task he shall be granted an opportunity to rescue his beloved wife from inter-dimensional flux. Trying in vain to find her way to warm bosom of Berlin she wanders the timestreams calling his name. Little does she know that she stands within the echoing hallways of devils.

Mrs Salbutamon appears on the inter-dimensional monitor as she walks through a tunnel like The Wizard of Oz/Labyrinth. *Then straight into the trick. This feat is performed 'against the clock' with the steamclock centrepiece beginning a countdown. Mr Salbutamon farts the names of novels – in what sounds like a strained human voice – while the pianist plays along, intermittently abusing Salbutamon and singing Eighties power ballads. There is a farting sound, then the novels' titles:* King Solomon's Mines, Fear and Loathing in Berlin *and the novelisation of the feature film* The Jewel in the Nile.

Pianist: Well done Salbutamon. Victory! The chance is yours ... quickly to the portal, pull her free, Barok has provided you with a rope. She is beyond the door! Hear her call your name! Do not surrender her to the Anti-Rooms of Misrule! Salbutamon! Quickly, the many-angled ones are stirring!

An inter-dimensional portal opens up as part of the stage. It's a bit like a gorilla's vagina; there's steam and lights and stuff coming out and two Pheenome use the rope to climb out of the dimension. Salbutamon pulls more rope out and his wife gets closer to the camera. The last tugs on the rope should smack his wife's face against the screen. The clock runs out and we see her spiralling back into the void. He falls back as the rope comes out of the opening. He lands on his back. We see he has pulled something out of the void.

Pianist: Well done, Mr Salbutamon. Your wife is being traded on the market of souls. Her price ... two groats. And a giant worm has entered this dimension, where it has begun to devour Time.

Traces of the netherworld remain. Salbutamon, your boobery snared the narrative of class struggle! In our physical vibration it has manifested as Glen Michael and Taggart locked in a mortal combat!

Glen Royalist, wearing a gaudy crown, rings etc., but hugely bearded and wearing rags, is holding a jewelled dagger to Taggart's throat. Meanwhile, Taggart is similarly dishevelled and wearing a necklace of chicken bones as he holds a sharpened chicken bone to Glen's throat.

Pianist: Ladies and Gentlemen, the patrons of tonight's performance have been Messr's Nestlé and Nestlé of Berlin. Providing purpose for the godless savages of the tropics.

Goodnight.

Just reading that back makes me think that we had lost it to drugs. In fact, it makes me think that I was a junkie and Jim was my imaginary friend. Glen Michael, I should explain, was a guy who presented a cartoon show in Scotland when we were kids. He actually appeared on the first series of *Live Floor Show*, popping up as a brief cutaway when Bob Doolally claimed to have been married to him. After the show he got up on stage and delivered quite a mental speech encompassing the nature of comedy and his own legacy. Pretty much exactly what you would have hoped for.

Another sketch I wrote with Jim for *Live Floor Show* included a character called Dr Presley. He was a sort of vainglorious rogue scientist who described himself as being at the centre of most of the world's conspiracy theories. He had a vaguely South

American air and was guided by a horrendous skull-faced monkey on his shoulder called Nando. His monologues were often him listing the reasons he was 'so fucking great':

'I have attracted flak for selling powdered milk to Africa. And African breastmilk to Tescos. My influence is such that I attempted to have my face carved on to the surface of Mars, only to find it was already there. I have learned to use 68 per cent of my brain power; I can design a new language everyday ... particularly one that consists only of harsh insults and requests for love making. I have files on everyone based on genetic probability factors so I can blackmail anyone before they have done the thing for which they are blackmailed in such a persuasive way as they become compelled to do the thing they are being black-mailed for.

'I conducted an experiment wherein I gathered 68 volunteers. They were paired at random; one member of each pair had a purple satin scarf bound over their eyes. They were getting a torch, a map, a radio and thirty minutes to negotiate a multi-levelled course of obstacles. 67 of them were eaten by a giant crab. I'm always saying it, but that's definitely the last time I conduct any experiments on ... GIANT CRAB ISLAND!!!'

Despite the fact that I talk about them a lot, I'm really scepti-cal of most conspiracy theories. I don't think the World Trade Center bombings were a CIA plot, or any of that stuff. I think the biggest mystery about the whole Diana thing was not whether or not she was murdered in a plot hatched by Prince Philip to prevent the future king's father-in-law from being a Muslim, but how did Mohammed Al-Fayed make so much money when he's clearly a fucking maniac!

People still think that Elvis faked his death. If he did, is it really likely he would have died in a shitting accident? If you faked your death you'd make it something brave – pushing a young girl out of the way of a lorry. Who'd fake their death as a jobby-related heart attack? That said, I have an open mind; I'm not the sort of person who believes everything he sees in the news. It's 30 years since Elvis's 'death'; 40 since we 'landed on the moon' and 80 since we discovered 'penicillin'. You would be shocked at some of the stuff I would be able to tell you if I was still alive.

Throughout these whole few years of being on Scottish telly I was living with a woman in Edinburgh. It was tempestuous, partly because I was always drugged and writing, partly because we were both nuts. She was an artist and did lots of drawings of me being beaten to death or being sexually abused by animals. Looking back, that probably wasn't a good sign. She was great, though, funny and creative, but it was never right between us and we struggled along like badly set bones.

We went to relationship counselling for a bit. One day I went on acid. I was talking to the counsellor about my childhood and looking out the window. The tenements facing us seemed to clench themselves into a giant stone fist.

I've since discovered one of the keys to a successful relationship is the ability to listen to what your other half did during the day and pretend you are not cripplingly bored. Nodding is good. As is the occasional 'Really?' If you hear a name you recognise take a stab at identifying them

'Is that Maggie that works on reception?'

'No, that's a different Maggie. Sometimes I wonder if you listen to me at all!'

Right or wrong you have 'taken an interest' and that's what matters. Annoyingly, your partner will often be interested in hearing about your day at work. A good tactic is to pretend you work in some secretive military job that you can't talk about.

It was at this point that two years of drug abuse began to have a cumulative effect. We made a sacrifice for success in our Dr Presley writing (a joint and a one pence piece) to a statue in the park. Afterwards we noticed that the statue had a tiny monkey on his shoulder and a jester's robe around his feet.

In the writing session that day, we seriously started to think that somehow we had managed to magic Dr Presley into actual existence in our reality, that escaping from his fictional prison was exactly the sort of thing he'd be trying to do, and that he was going to fuck us up badly. We had taken pills with the horse tranquilliser ketamine in them, which I don't think helped.

We wrote a sketch for the show where Jim played Dr Presley and I was Dr Presley 36, a version of the Doctor from another dimension. The sketch started with Dr Presley cutting my throat quite horribly. He then goes on to deliver a truly mental monologue that I can't believe found its way onto national TV. It detailed the various reasons that he 'is so fucking great' and every so often the Doctor would make the whole room shake with his bizarre mental powers.

Of course it's ridiculous to think that the Doctor could have made the leap into our reality or started to fuck with us. I split up with my girlfriend that week. As she told me she was leaving, the show started on the TV over her shoulder. She dropped the news as I was watching the doctor slash my throat from end to end.

I was in quite a weird place after the break-up and had a few one-night stands, something I'd not really done before. I got off with the oldest woman I've ever slept with. Older women are underrated. The sex is great and they'll often tidy your room afterwards. And you never miss *Emmerdale*. Actually, this lady was maybe only 42, but it seemed pretty old at the time. It was great actually; we both got high and went at it with that abandon you have when there's nothing to lose. I'm not proud of this, but I couldn't manage to come, and to try to get myself to come I focussed on a picture of her on her bedside table where she was much younger. It felt like I was trying to push my cock back through time. In the photo she was standing on a pier on holiday holding a big fish she'd caught. Still, it worked.

We had both taken a big ecstasy tablet I'd never seen before. It was enormous and looked sort of like one of those old Refreshers sweeties. Anyway, if you ever see one, take it; we were high and shagging for about two days. It was nuts; her gynaecologist will have thought that she'd been hit by a car. Eventually, we ordered a pizza and watched a movie. It was *A Perfect Storm*, that George Clooney tuna movie. It says a lot about that film that even high on ecstasy, eating pizza beside a beautiful woman I was going to fuck before and afterwards, it was still shit. I hope they use that sentence as a quote on the DVD box.

It sort of ended badly because she had this shelf of books under the TV. It contained every commercial book that you'd seen people reading on a train for the previous few years: *Captain Corelli's Mandolin* and so on. I thought it was an ironic statement, a sort of joke, and complimented her on what I took to be some kind of artistic critique about the mundanity of modern culture. It transpired that this was her actual library and our utter incompatibility was suddenly obvious. Still, it was fun. Two days may actually be the perfect length for a relationship.

That was the only period of my life where I shagged around, and I learned quite a lot. For instance, role-play is great. There's nothing makes sex better with a chick than spending a couple of years pretending to be her long-lost brother. I also learned not to date women you meet through your friends. You don't want to find out what your friends' lives are like. I couldn't go partying with Andy all night once I knew he had kids, and that his name was Andy.

I ignored the idea that you are supposed to find out somebody's history before becoming intimate. Ask your partner about their sexual history before you fuck them? It's hard enough trying to forget my own. The last thing I want to hear before sex is a fucking roll call. You listen to someone's whole sex life, you'll rather stick your dick in a red-hot meteor. I know they can't cure

HIV, but how hard would it be to come up with something that meant you could taste it on people's saliva? It'll mean that most people with HIV will never develop AIDS. They'll choke to death on Tic Tacs.

Eventually, I managed to get a good friend of mine pregnant. We were both pretty pleased about it and ended up with a beautiful daughter. I had always wanted a girl. I found out that it was a girl when we had a scan the day before the birth. I was walking home through the park and, after having a good look around to check nobody was there, skipped across the bridge.

It's going to be interesting being a full-time dad in a few years, and finding out just how boring my kids find me. There's so much information and distractions these days that kids get bored easily. In my day if someone found a porn mag it would circulate around the school for weeks. By the time you got a loan of it, it would be like trying to look at something encased in amber.

I think being a parent is the ultimate responsibility. People label somebody like Amy Winehouse self-destructive, but I blame her parents. Especially her mum. She's the one that must have fucked a horse. Angelina Jolie is often described as the most beautiful woman in the world. Yet after so many kids she must have vag like a rubbish chute. Susan Boyle's vagina on Angelina's body, now that's what I'm talking about. Scientists, there's a *Frankie Boyle Live* DVD to the first to deliver.

I hated being at the birth, having always found hospitals creepy. Luckily my daughter's mum had to have quite a lot of drugs so I nipped out for a couple of hours in the middle and watched a football match without her realising.

Childbirth is many things, but it is not sexy. Even though I once turned the volume down and masturbated to a birth on the Open University. For one thing, there's the stretchmarks. Your partner's beautiful, alabaster stomach will end up looking like a school desk in a remedial class.

That said, I've always had a grim fascination with horrible medical stuff. Earlier this year an Australian doctor performed brain surgery on a 13-year-old boy with a household power drill. He said the trickiest part of the operation was attaching the mahogany book shelves. And did you see that an American woman called Connie had a face transplant? Apparently the surgeon used to work on *Bo' Selecta!* Obviously this transplant makes Connie happy, but somewhere a sumo wrestler's wife is grieving. Connie says this face transplant means she 'can blend into the crowd'. She's moving to Scotland?

I think nowadays I'd be worried about the whole MRSA thing. A man who committed suicide was found in a locked hospital toilet where he had lain for three days. A source at the hospital said, 'It makes you wonder what the cleaners were doing.' Have you seen the state of the toilets in a hospital? He probably was the cleaner. Any cleaner that found him would just have stuck a Pine Fresh toilet block in his mouth and a toilet roll on his dick.

FOURTEEN

Live Floor Show was given a network series, but the producer dropped me, replacing me with a good-looking black guy. I don't blame the producer for this; he had a good reason. He knew fuck-all about comedy. Jim and Craig were still on the show though, so I got a job writing for both of them. It was good to be out of performing for a bit and a relief to think of ideas without having to worry about how you were going to sell them. In fact, you had the amusement of watching other people worry about it.

I had a little more time on my hands, so I taught myself to swim. None of your fancy lessons either; with sheer will-power I had developed my own powerful idiosyncratic style. It had the added benefit of encouraging people in the pool to avoid me. Now that I had some time off performing I just swam all the time. Scotland's municipal pools have an every-man-for-himself atmosphere, like the D-Day landings in Speedos. I toured the pools, swimming almost everywhere in Glasgow. There was one in Giffnock where everybody was so old it was like a scene from *Cocoon*. I tried the pool in Clydebank on a day where everybody was mentally impaired. I couldn't work out if this was a special day or just what people are like in Clydebank.

There was a pool near my house where they'd pack them in like the ending of *Titanic*. It had a truly mental sauna where people would sell knock-off DVDs, eat oranges, shave and exchange spirited abuse. I once heard two brothers musing on where their pitbull saw them in the pack pecking order.

'My auld man thinks he's number wan! The dog humps his leg – he canny be number wan! Ahm number wan!'

Trust me, if you're worrying about where you are in your dog's preferences, the dog is number one.

There was an older guy, a muscular tattooed maniac who'd come in a lot. One night somebody said to him:

'Hey Jamesy! I hear you were playing Davie's lot at five-a-side the other night. How'd you get on?'

'How did I get on?' roared Jamesy. 'Ah punched him and ah punched his brother!'

I joined a posh sauna in the West End but it was boring; lawyers talking about their tax bills and mortgages. Nobody had ever punched anybody and his brother. I'm still at a private gym, which I feel a bit bad about. On the other hand, I just couldn't take the shiteness of the municipal places anymore. I was always greeted by some world-weary poster boy for autism, staring blankly over my shoulder as he told me I couldn't swim because it was women's day, or because it was Tuesday, or because everything was broken. In my new gym they've trained someone attractive to tell me that everything is broken with a smile.

Learning to swim obviously did nothing to improve my fitness. I did a radio series that was a travelogue of the West Highland Way. There were five or six of us presenting it, including wee Sandy Nelson, walking the 95 miles between Glasgow and Fort

William. None of us made it. It started off as a daytime show, as it was supposed to be a cheery travel piece, but once the gruelling catalogue of failure was edited it got renamed *Fear and Loathing on the West Highland Way* and put out at midnight.

My angle was to go without doing any preparation and to not take any stuff. I literally didn't even bring a coat. Jimmy McGregor, the Scottish celebrity walker, turned up to see us off and do a wee interview when we started in Milngavie. It says a lot about Scotland that we have a celebrity walker, and he was horrified at my approach. He was stunned that I was just leaving with the clothes I had on me and a Mars bar. I would find stuff along the way, making it more of an adventure, I assured him.

I did find stuff. We tried to walk it in five days and I found a pair of rubber overtrousers someone had left on a hedge, a hat and gloves. It was like being one of the Wombles. Or a tramp. None of us had any experience of that kind of walking and after the first day we all moaned like fuck. After two days a couple of the presenters started hitching. Myself and Sandy kept going. On day three we felt pretty good and ran a big downhill section. It was incredibly exhilarating bouncing from rock to rock, wondering if you could actually stop. On day four I realised that I had wrecked my knee doing that. I tried to do the last day limping up the final hilly bit but some irate outdoor types told me I was in no fit state and politely told me to fuck off from their mountain. I got a bus back to Glasgow, failing miserably at a physical challenge regularly completed by the elderly, fat Americans and the terminally ill.

Fresh from the failure of the walk, I hit on another plan – this time to visit bothies and connect with the real Scotland for a Hunter S. Thompson-esque column I was writing for a Scottish newspaper. But this came off the rails in a spectacular fashion. The first stop was Cumbernauld. Cumbernauld was once described as the 'most dismal' town in the whole of Scotland. Whoever thinks Cumbernauld is the most dismal town in Scotland obviously hasn't travelled around much. Cumbernauld is the most dismal town in the whole of the world. Next stop was Inverary, but we couldn't find the bothy we'd planned to stay in and then couldn't get a room at the hotel. Maybe they were genuinely full on a Monday night, or maybe it was the fact that I looked like I'd just been dragged off the bottom of a riverbed. We ploughed on to Oban. On a Monday, it has the overall atmosphere of a tramp's funeral. We went into an old-man's pub in the centre, put a lot of Barry Manilow and reggae on the jukebox, and danced incongruously in a bar cramped with dour-faced hillwalkers. There's something in the way we all bend our necks to capitalism that meant, just because I had put a pound in the jukebox, nobody punched me for making them listen to a disco remix of 'Copacabana'. In a saner world, I would now be lying drowned in a lobster pot.

People always ask why Scottish tourism struggles. Because it's an amazingly expensive, wet and unfriendly country. For the price of two days in Mull and Oban we could easily have had a week in Spain. Maybe Spanish people are unfriendly too – I don't know because I can't understand a word they're saying.

That said, small businesses in Scotland have apparently been far less affected by the recession than firms in England and Wales, thus proving, whatever the climate, there will always be an American willing to pay for a document proving that the surname Goldberg really has a clan tartan.

Later we went and sat in the cathedral. We thought it was totally empty until we worked out that there was a priest sitting in a wee wooden box, waiting for people to come in and confess to stuff. The whole thing gave me an enormous sexual thrill. I wish I'd had the guts to go in and confess that to him. The next day, I ran into a guy who – over the course of a rambling chat – offered to do some design stuff for posters I needed for a festival I was doing. Nice fella. It only occurred to me on the way home that he was clearly gay and had been hitting on me. I pulled the email address he had given me out of my pocket. I don't know that I'll be getting in touch with spunkymark@hotmail.com.

One thing I did learn from the trip was that there seems to be a conspiracy not to mention the fact that Scotland is a rubbish place to have a holiday. Glasgow has a 'tour bus' that has so little to show people it seems to spend about ten minutes on the motorway. That's got to be a challenge for the guide to keep talking.

'And if you look to your right just now you should be able to see … a Renault Clio. And if you look very carefully out your left hand window, you should see … your own reflection in the glass.'

I can understand why we'd talk it up to gullible tourists (to poochle their foreign money), but why should we lie to each other? The only way a campaign to persuade Scots to holiday in Scotland could be successful would be if it had the slogan 'Visit Scotland ... Spain's been hit by a nuclear bomb.'

Desperate to escape and have a proper holiday, I went to see Celtic in the UEFA Cup Final in Seville. It was bonkers. The whole city just partying fans, with the locals having wisely fled into the hills. Seville was beautiful and I had a great time. I couldn't book a hotel room anywhere but just wandered into a five-star hotel somewhere and slept in a little roofless garden, curled up round the base of a big cactus with the stars up above me.

The drinking really shocked me though, and so did the physical condition of the fans. Everyone was waddling about in XXL Celtic tops. There were guys who looked like they'd just stuck their head out of the top of a duvet cover. I was standing on a corner talking to some forty-somethings and made a joke about the A-Team and nobody knew what I was talking about. They were too young. These were guys in their early twenties and they looked like they were dying under a witch's curse.

It really brought it home to me that we are an alcoholic country. Perhaps some friendly nation will one day make an intervention, invade us and police our streets with a UN Gripekeeping Force. I sometimes wonder what we could achieve as a country if we just gave up the drugs and booze. Look at all the stuff we invented in the past: TV; tarmacadam; capitalism; and, according to a drunk I met at a party, Motown. England came up with nothing. They were too busy working on the copyright and patenting system.

I think our nation's health problems are partly down to the massive inequality in Scotland. I read a report recently that showed the regions in Glasgow with the highest and lowest life expectancies are separated by just a few miles. One area sees people living well into their 80s, while the other has a life expectancy of 57, lower than Iraq. I don't think Scots particularly mind having a lower life expectancy than Iraq; it's the lower standard of football that really grates. After all, if you live here you'll know that 57 years feels like plenty. Glasgow's Lord Provost was said to be slightly surprised by the news, causing him to have a massive heart attack. A report like that could be a chance for Scotland to change its ways. But it won't. I'd be surprised if it hasn't already been used as roach paper. We will take this report on board as the average Scottish male takes advice from his doctor, with a pinch of salt – and a dab of speed. Maybe some Valium if he can score off the doctor.

Later that year, Jim and I were signed up to do a show at the Edinburgh Festival. We'd both have much rather donated our still-attached balls to medical science. We'd now done loads of telly in Scotland, but knew there was still no way we'd be able to attract an audience from the sort of cunts who go to the festival. We went through a brief, drug-fuelled period of wanting to do it as two nightmarish golf buddies, sort of like an evil Bob Hope and Bing Crosby. We'd go to a driving range stoned and write gags about the movies these guys had done together. It really made me laugh. We did a couple of previews and nobody knew what the fuck we were talking about, so it was back to stand-up.

I'd known for a while I'd be doing that year's Edinburgh Festival after a dream I'd had. I dreamt that I was drowning in an ocean of burning shit and I knew what it meant. I've since asked my agent who makes all the money at the Fringe. She showed me a photograph of a spaceship half-buried in a quarry and I never asked again.

Edinburgh is a giant tourist trap. It's really a collection of kilt shops with a bus network. Everyone there either works in banking or sells Arran sweaters; now even the RBS HQ is just a gift shop selling musical sporrans. The recent economic collapse has hit the city hard. Edinburgh was miserable during the boom years – with the collapse of the banks it's become like a Leonard Cohen song with planning permission.

When the festival arrives so does the Fringe. The festival regards the Fringe like a dog turd it just can't shake off its wing-tipped brogues. They know while they're attending the premier of *The Cherry Orchard* in Swahili thousands are watching a man shitting light bulbs on the Royal Mile for free, and having much more fun. Comedy at the Fringe used to be a fun pick'n'mix. You could watch stand-up in an abandoned church for under a fiver. Now it's a massive corporate bumfest. Edinburgh Council charges so much for venues, most comedians have to wear 'Golf Sale' signs during gigs to break even. Money and sponsorship ruin everything. Before long some comedians will do their show from inside a giant KFC bucket on the roof of a rotating Mazda coupé. They're already talking about a 'Fringe Fringe'. Good. Then we can get back to watching Norwegian improv in a derelict foot clinic.

Remember to cherish your homegrown Scottish performers at the Fringe. They lead briefer, unhappier lives than other comics but burn all the brighter for it, like a mayfly or a jobby in a bonfire. It's also good to see Glaswegian punters at the Fringe. With the world's biggest arts festival just round the corner, it must be difficult to tear yourself away from murdering a neighbour in a dispute about a satellite dish. For a lot of Glaswegians, going to the Edinburgh Fringe is like visiting the snobbiest person you know while they're hosting a dinner party for a troupe of contemporary dancers. So well done to all the Scottish people who travel there to the festival; you are still the only people in the world who are watching opera drunk.

Edinburgh is full of mainly white, middle-class Presbyterians. I suppose if you're told every Sunday that laughter is the sound of Satan farting then you're not really going to be a bundle of laughs. I was thrown out of Edinburgh's City Café for having my friend's children with me. Despite being a supposedly cosmopolitan bar in the centre of the world's biggest arts festival, they simply don't want to have children in their establishment. This is not unusual in Scotland – publicans are generally worried that the sound of children's laughter will remind their customers that there is a world outside grim-faced drinking. It also comes from a deeply ingrained sexism – children should be at home with their mums, men should be in the pubs drinking in peace. If you're going by the City Café, why not pop in and tell them what you think if you're a parent. Or even better, a dangerously paranoid schizophrenic. Listen carefully. I think that's God telling you to go and have a word.

Being in a show that's going badly often brings it home how little other people really know about what you're doing. Because something's going badly, people will sometimes feel a bit freer about offering you their advice. We had a meeting with Jim's agent after one performance and he told us that 'the opening jokes didn't go great. Perhaps you needed to write some stronger stuff for the top.' Those are our best jokes, we told him, they just aren't working here. 'Is what you're saying,' asked Jim, 'that the show would be better if we wrote some more jokes that were better than our best jokes?' The guy beamed, glad to have got his message across.

We were both in a strange place, doing something we didn't really want to be doing. The show was a reflection of our grim state of mind. We wrote a bit that I really liked for the Reverend about how a lot of show-business gays have had 'an Ass-child. Fifty per cent gay faeces and fifty per cent gay semen makes an Ass-child. You know Frankie Muniz from *Malcolm in the Middle*? Bruce Willis's Ass-child. He denied it at first but his DNA was found on scrapings taken from the end of Demi Moore's cock.'

My favourite bit from that show was the Reverend's book he'd written to help people better understand the AIDS virus. It was called *How I Beat the Gay Rabies: Three Years Living in a Steel Cube Buried in the Desert*.

I started doing a bit at the end of the show called 'Thought for the Day'. I'd come on in one of the costumes hanging in the dressing room and shout jokes from a book in a weird staccato English voice. For a while I'd wear a costume that had a sort of Renaissance gentleman feel to it, from a one-man show called *The Fisher King*. The Fisher King came along one night and saw this, leaving behind a note telling me sternly not to do it again and signed 'The Fisher King'.

There was a peculiarity in that I could get jokes to work in that voice which never worked in my own. They were sort of prosey jokes. My favourite was:

'I have a thought about army training. The real training for any soldier in the British Army is not the six weeks that he spends at camp, but the seventeen years that he lives on a housing estate. The moment of epiphany for any soldier is the first time that he is punched in the stomach by his commanding officer. And he realises that his father had been pulling his punches, and had loved him all along.'

Perhaps you need to see me saying it with a beard in a World War I uniform. The last joke in the show was always:

'I have a thought about sexual politics. Why is it that when I find a vibrator in my girlfriend's drawer, she's liberated? Yet when she looks in the chest that I keep under my bed and finds an artificial vagina, I'm a pervert? So what if it is a dog's vagina that I keep alive with batteries.'

The one night we sold out we did the most disastrous thing we could have done. We gave the final ten minutes of the show over to doing a thing called 'Jools Holland's Tiny Hootenanny'. This involved having toys on the stage arranged as little bands. We'd introduce them as various bands and then we'd play a CD of their biggest number, produced to sound like a tiny, high-pitched voice was singing it. I think it was as a doll of The Mighty Thor sang Norah Jones that everybody walked out.

I've never really felt any sense of kinship with other comedians; they've always seemed too needy. I don't think I need the love, approval, affirmation, whatever it is, that other people are after. Maybe I did at the start of my career; I can't remember because I was drunk. At that festival a fire alarm went off during one of the shows and the building got evacuated. Everybody was doing their shows in the courtyard. The show had to go on. We just slunk off with our hoods up, glad of a night off. I don't think it's entirely about me being a miserable bastard. Stand-up needs a roof and a microphone, and I'm not so desperate for love that I'll yell my jokes out in a car park, like a cunt. God only know how hard those guys' dads must have been able to punch.

I never read reviews anymore, not mine or anybody else's. It really depresses me how much attention comics pay to that stuff. 100 words that the classical music critic's wife writes for gin money can make or break somebody's year. That's clearly ridiculous and a position that any intelligent person should be able to think their way out of. If you want an opinion, invite somebody you respect and ask them what they thought. Comedy criticism is basically what a cunt thought of something they didn't understand. I know a comic who did a show called *Beyond the Pale:*

100 Years of Irish History, basically a potted history of Ireland, and it was very good. He told me that his main review that year said that he went on about Ireland a bit too much. That's the level of most comedy criticism. It's amusingly shit I suppose, but sad for anyone who actually takes it seriously.

Jimmy Carr saw us at the festival and gave us a job writing for him on his quiz show *Distraction*. Even then, Jimmy was at an echelon of show business that we could only dream of. He had access to drugs that allowed him to speak almost any language and could teleport at will. We've got to know him socially since, and he's a lovely chap. Most of his time is spent in a huge *Lawnmower Man*-style machine with Jonathan Ross. He says that they use it to commune with aliens and occasionally make love, but knowing him as I do it must be something infinitely more sinister. There are rumours that it's part of a plot by Jimmy to re-imagine the earth in the shape of his own face. At least it will be bigger.

I think for *Distraction* we had to write jokes based on the biographies of the appalling people they chose as contestants. These were generally beery rughy blokes or sex-case tour reps. Looking at the details of their 'lives' was like peeking under a rock. I say 'I think' because we were desperately stoned at the time. Jimmy might have been presenting the news for all I know.

I stopped smoking dope after that. When you finally get off drugs, the world seems like a much less threatening place. I ran into my old crystal-meth buddy the other day. Turns out that the talking cat from outer space was just a movie we saw when we were high. Actually, there's a lot of nonsense talked about drugs. They don't make you paranoid. That's an idea the CIA injected into our culture through hidden messages in *Happy Days*.

I found it quite hard to finally give everything up. The way your body keeps craving stuff. Thank God I never took cocaine. It's amazing how extreme the physical reaction is to withdrawal. My body would have turned into a missile that fired itself at Colombia. Jim kept going and these days the only way he can get enough tranquillisers to come down is to dress up as an escaped lion and jump around in the cafeteria of the local zoo.

The main reason I stopped smoking dope was that it started to give me a crippling, overwhelming fear of my own mortality. I remember it hitting me with total clarity that I am going to die and everybody I know is going to die too. I was sitting having a joint in the afternoon, watching a home-improvement show when the reality of death crushed all interest in the conservatory of a sexually ambiguous project manager. Mortality is a good thing to face up to. I reckon people meditate for years to achieve what I had right then, a frenzied, disabling horror. Looking down at my legs I could see the muscles twitching in a classic flight response. My legs were trying to run away while my brain grimly reminded them that there was no outrunning this thing. A fact that *OK!* magazine wanted to remind Jade Goody of when they dedicated 'an official tribute' issue to her earlier this year. The only trouble being they did it while she was still alive. This must have been shocking to Jade, particularly as the obituary explained she died in a motorcycling accident while trying to jump twelve London buses. That sounds like a good idea for a new reality-television show. Terminally ill people are given obituaries written by the public which they have to enact as accurately as possible to win money for the people they leave behind. You can imagine Noel Edmonds: '... Next up on *Suddenly/Peaceful* we'll have Maureen, 95, who needs to die in a circus-tent fire, as she attempts the world's first display of flaming midget juggling.'

Poor Jade Goody. If you were going to guess her final words, surely they would have been along the lines of asking her children to take good care of her husband. She said she was looking forward to going to heaven; unfortunately she thought that heaven was a region of Portugal. I missed the reports from the funeral, but luckily for quite a while her coffin cam was screening footage through the night on E4. Of course, we've all fantasised about our own funeral, wondering how sad everybody we know will be, having that girl we always loved turning up distraught, leaping from the coffin as a zombie and becoming Ground Zero for the death of humanity. Wendy Richard was buried in an eco-friendly coffin woven from bamboo. I'm planning on doing the same as that's how I'd like to go. Ripped apart by ravenous pandas.

Inspired by our time writing for *Distraction*, Jim and I went into a kind of development hell working on a pilot with Craig Hill for BBC Scotland. There was a real tension between BBC Scotland wanting us to do a basic, shitty show with jokes about Scotland and us, well, not really wanting to.

One of the main battles was our desire to have a guest host, Fish from Marillion, which they eventually let us do. Fish was great. He just didn't give a fuck and did whatever gags we asked him to. He opened with 'Hello people of Scotland. We know that you won't be watching this if you're in Dundee, you'll be outside date-raping a seagull.' Fish was also our interviewee in an item called 'Jungle Bus', where we were to interview celebrities every week on a bus full of mercenaries, fighting its way through the African jungle. We'd do the interview, while the celebrity helped us man a roof-mounted machine gun, and then we'd kick them out of the bus with a small scrap of map, and they would be immediately murdered by the natives.

I don't think I can really explain how much the commissioning editor hated this show. I had a character who was a revolutionary from the Spanish Civil War and he asked me if I could make him a Scottish janitor. That's the kind of gulf we're talking about. We made it during winter, which is always a mistake in Scotland. People we knew and had worked with before just acted like they'd been replaced by alien seed pods. Cunty alien seed pods.

My favourite bit of the show was a thing we all wrote with Jim. I think we were all on Valium for the writing sessions, which gave it a weird prosey quality. It was a monologue by an overblown, Jerry Bruckheimer-style movie producer called T. Carter Mondell. Here he is:

I like all pictures to come in under twenty words, including the words I speak. That's ten. What? A man in a house? What kind of shit idea is that? Can't the house be a prison and the man be a vampire?

I feel that I have a lot more energy than a lot of people in Hollywood because I'm not a fag pretending not to be a fag. That's gotta take up a whole lot of time. Attempted assassinations? I've not lost a lot of sleep over that, just a few wives and a child.

Dennis Hopper liked to challenge himself at the end of every take. He would drink a bottle of Scotch and smash himself in the forehead with a mallet. The challenge was to remember his lines. He forgot his lines. He also forgot what movie he was in, who he was, where he was and what he was. He would start screaming a number that he claimed was the key to the universe. We learned later it was the telephone number of a local head surgeon.

Phil Spector was doing a cameo as a bagman till he fashioned a tree out of cocaine and it fell on him. The crew were great friends with Phil Spector, despite the fact that he was always trying to murder them. Every morning he dived out of his trailer spraying bullets across the set. People were surprised when they heard that he killed a woman. What surprised me was that he did it with a gun. He always insisted that if he got the opportunity he'd do it with a golf club. I had my doubts about Phil since I saw him masturbating at the O. J. Simpson trial.

Roman Polanski didn't move to Europe because of a rape charge. He moved because the standard of living over in the States is so high that he could no longer overpower the average 13 year old.

They sent a stripper to my room. I thought it was one of the hookers that you're allowed to beat. That's what I ordered. She's suing me for assault and battery, and I am counter-suing to be allowed to come in her ears.

Wherever the conflict in your movie set is, you need to send a white guy in. A black hero? As far as Joe Schmo's concerned, you might as well rub black cum in his daughter's face or have some black guy blow his windows in with black sperm in a drive-by from his pump-action black balls.

You've got to make movies about the stuff that people want to see. What people really want to see is chicks in sports bras being stabbed by a psycho. Have you seen the African version of Rainman, where the boy is taken into a clearing and has his head smashed by rocks? He never learns to count. The rest of the film is about Mseste Mtbmu's desperate search for food and water.

People ask me where do I get my ideas for my movies – I drive out into the Mohave Desert, sit upon the mesa and smoke a combination of herbs and gekko sweat, then I go into a deep meditative state and enter the

Dreamtime where I open all of my senses to the rhythms of the universe – then I drive back to my office and read the scripts I've been sent. I gotta real knack for developing scripts. I remember this writer comes to me and says he's got an idea for a romantic comedy set against a backdrop of racial oppression – I had the vision to take that script and make Full Moon Lockdown. Another time I got a script for a road movie. A middle-aged guy discovers he's got two teenage daughters and takes them on a road trip of discovery across America. Right away I knew I had found the movie I'd waited all my life to make – Full Moon Lockdown 3.

I remember a script lands on my desk this one time. It was for a movie about a team of US commandos that fly into South America to take down a scientist who's threatening to unleash an army of zombie soldiers. It was like the writer was reading my mind. I took his script and made Terms of Endearment 2. I see my movies like I see my children, at weekends in cinemas.

This is a business ... show business. Sometimes the business of making money, arranging for a certain race of hooker to be placed in Jean-Claude Van Damme's camper van, sometimes arranging for the body of a certain race of hooker to be removed from J-CVD's camper van. And sometimes it's about making movies.

The thing I look for in a movie is Entertainability ... does it have the ability to entertain? Or not? I'm not asking, 'Does this movie move me? Are the characters well developed? Is it relevant to my life?' I want it to be the biggest, loudest piece of shit I've seen this week. Other than my kid.

You know what makes ideas great? Cocaine. If they sold it with your popcorn this shit would make a lot more sense to you. Wesley Snipes was so desperate to be famous he allowed us to make him black. And call him Wesley. Thanks for eating my ass, Wo-Ling-Ho.

I take a gun with me everywhere because you never know who you'll have to shoot. It's part of my therapy to shoot my reflection three times a day.

I get some of my best ideas during heart attacks. You think you've lived? Unless you've had a heart attack inside Uma Thurman's ass, you've never lived.

I put forward the concept of a movie that would be a 120-minute shot of a vagina. They said it would alienate our female audience. I said make it Sarah Jessica Parker's vagina and get her shoes in the shot. People say I see women as sex objects ... I don't. I see them as a life-support system for a vagina. I say to women, 'Your vagina's not losing its self-respect. Your vagina's not got any dignity, your vagina doesn't feel any shame. Just butt out and let us get on with it. It has nothing to do with you. Your only responsibility is not to die during this.'

A director once told me I was decadent. I came in his ears and beat him to death with a peacock.

That experience convinced me that I'd need to go down south to do telly stuff. There was a whole circuit of what are called 'office pilots' in London, where production companies film tasters of shows in their offices. I hadn't quite made the move to live there full time so I was skint for a year, and often playing quite ill-conceived games in front of an audience of jaded researchers. I remember one where we had to do jokes about what random celebrities might say at their moment of orgasm. I went into a hysterical laughing fit thinking about how much funnier it would be to grab the producer in a headlock and jump out of the window.

For a long time I always stayed in the same hotel in London. The Russians who worked there all got to know me and started to anticipate my idiotic needs. It was a bit like being the Major in *Fawlty Towers*. It was always good looking into the glassy eyes of the sinister Russian duty manager knowing that a man who may well have killed to get his passport was in charge of finding me an ironing board. One night it sounded like a bunch of staff came into the room next to mine and gangbanged a Russian woman against the adjoining door. There were a lot of nods and winks the next day. That's when you know you've become over-familiar in a hotel. When the staff are staging group-sex pranks to keep you awake. I acted mildly irritated, but had obviously found it all pretty horny, and had a tempestuous wank that comfortably makes my all-time Top Ten.

I don't understand London's racism toward Eastern Europeans. I don't have a problem with a Polish plumber coming round to do work on my house. They're cheap, arrive on time and it's a lot easier to understand what they're saying than a British workman. I had a Polish worker round at my house last week, and I was more than happy with the service ... they knew exactly what they were doing, they were thorough, cleaned up afterwards, and she didn't have that dead look behind her eyes that you normally get from British prostitutes.

One of the things I tried out for was *Mock the Week*. It was quite impressions-orientated when they came up with it, because Rory Bremner was on it. I couldn't do any impressions so I didn't think I'd be in it if it got made. It was good to see Dara O Briain again; I'd been a fan since I'd worked with him in clubs years before. He used to have a really sinister bit where he'd pick a big guy in the audience to shake hands with and then just refuse to let go, as tension mounted. There's a wonderful juxtaposition in seeing such a delicate, tricksy mind contained in such an enormous body. I see him as being like a French nineteenth-century lady, a wit of some great lady's salon, who through early scientific endeavour has managed to have her brain transplanted into a gorilla.

While I was waiting to hear back about *Mock the Week*, I got a job writing for Jimmy Carr on *8 out of 10 Cats*. I think it was the first and only job that I really loved. Everybody was really nice. The other writers were better than me so the jokes got written whether I tried or not, and people went out and got you cake. The basic engine of the writers' room, the fuel that it ran on, was misogyny. We would take that energy, the desire to hurt women, and turn it into pithy monologues about statistics. The whole experience left me more convinced than ever that sex offenders should be forced to write hundreds of topical jokes per week, to dissipate their fell desires.

It was great that people went out and got you food, but we all started to get badly out of shape. Once we had somebody go to Greggs. I ate four chocolate doughnuts and an apple turnover. I went for a sauna that evening and started tripping; it felt like I could zoom my vision into extreme close-up, like a powerful photographic lens. We all kept talking about having an 'abs challenge', the idea being that knowing we'd have to display ourselves to the office meant we'd get rid of our bellies. We all secretly knew that our devotion to Nando's would have made any such contest a blasphemous obscenity. I think Jimmy would win that nowadays as he has lost quite a lot of weight. Sadly none of it off his head, so he looks like a fucking Pez dispenser.

Recently, I was doing a guest appearance on a show and ran into one of the guys I'd worked with on *Cats*. He told me about a joke they'd written about the Special Olympics that hadn't got in. 'At the Special Olympics this week, somebody was injured during the hammer throwing. But nobody could work out who it was.' Somehow that really made me miss them all.

FIFTEEN

Shortly after landing the job writing for Jimmy Carr, a couple of the shows I'd been trying out for actually got made. One was *FAQ U*, a sort of topical discussion thingy on Channel 4, and the other was *Mock the Week*. *FAQ U* was made in Bristol, so I had to go and live there for three weeks, nesting in a hotel bedroom that I turned into a masturbation furnace. I was a writer for the episodes that I wasn't on and wrote jokes for Justin Lee Collins, who struck me as being both a really nice guy and the opposite of talented. He looked just like the lion from *The Wizard of Oz* and we'd all keep trying to get Bert Lahr, the name of that actor, into the script out of boredom.

I was pretty surprised to hear that *Mock the Week* was getting made and that I was in it. It was welcome news. I'd bought a flat in Scotland to be near my daughter and was largely broke. Most of the regular guys who're on it now were about from the start. Dara and Hugh were on every week, and Andy Parsons popped up regularly. Russell Howard hadn't yet appeared but he was becoming increasingly popular across Britain for a series of unbelievable stunts on rocket-powered rollerskates, and it was getting more and more difficult for the producers to ignore him.

It was interesting to get to know all those guys and to have my eyes opened to the world of the big-league TV comics. Every regular on the show is as obsessed with showing off their martial-arts abilities as they are with flaunting their bisexuality. Hugh Dennis will regularly warm up for shows by stripping naked and throwing kickboxing combinations that stop inches from my face as I try to tear my gaze from his incongruous black genitals.

Andy Parsons is even more extreme. He stands in the wings waiting to go on and insists that everybody smash things off his tensed abdominals. Once I hit him with a chair until my hands were sore and he didn't make a sound, tears running silently down his amused face. Nobody enjoys this part of the build-up, not even Andy.

Dara is a man of gigantic mirths and gigantic melancholies. Often he will parade a woman around the green room who he insists is his mistress. It is perfectly obvious to everybody that it is several large joints of meat that Dara has sewn together. Nonetheless, we are all expected to show deference to this chimera, paying her compliments and kissing her sausage fingers when introduced. Occasionally, we are introduced to the 'child' of this blasphemous union. Dressed in the immaculate uniform of a top boys' school, it is clearly a Staffordshire bull terrier. Relentlessly questioned by the terrified production crew about its hobbies and hopes for the future as Dara gazes balefully on, the poor thing looks demented.

One of the peculiarities of panel-show comedy is the way that we are all expected and encouraged to shout over each other. On many shows you are given Red Bulls in your dressing room, sometimes even on set, without asking. I often think it must be

weird for the viewers to see a bunch of people screaming witti-
cisms as their hearts thrum in their chests like dying budgerigars.
I have long accepted the real possibility that I will have a massive
stroke while guesting on a David Mitchell-hosted celebrity news
quiz. Slabbering and palsied, I will still attempt to drool out some
funny reasons why something may or may not be the odd one
out while everybody shrieks over the top of me like the sound-
track to a monkey gangbang.

Then I was awarded perhaps the ultimate accolade: a gig on
Belgian TV. *Mock the Week* is shown on some late-night channel
so I am vaguely recognisable on the streets of Belgium. You read
that right. I hope it has made you pause to consider what you
have achieved with your own life.

I was met at the airport by a guy who looked exactly like
Antoine de Caunes, in a Fiat with his beautiful boyish assistant.
As we sped off through the thick fog he played 'You Spin Me
Right Round' at full volume as we all stared ahead impassively.
It was the most intensely European experience I had ever had.

One of the producers took me for lunch with some friends of
his. They were really great, incredibly friendly people on that
show. Over lunch they started laughing about all the stereotypes
there are about Scottish and English people and how there were
no stereotypes about Belgians. I was startled. 'But there are!
Everybody says that Belgians are boring ...' There was a collec-
tive wince. They looked genuinely crushed at this information and
started talking to each other in worried Dutch. They even called
over a friend from another table and imparted the harrowing

update. He took it like a bereavement. I was glad I hadn't got to finish my sentence, which was going to be 'Everybody says that Belgians are boring paedophiles.'

I'd come over a few days early for the show, to have a bit of a holiday. On the first night I managed to contract horrendous food poisoning and lay in my hotel room for three days hallucinating. Somehow there were mosquitoes in the room and they fed on my drugged, sleeping face. That's how I ended up appearing on a Dutch-language television show feeling mentally ill and with a face so swollen by insect bites that it resembled a baseball catcher's mitt. My memories of it are quite dreamlike. I had to listen carefully for my introduction and ran on after hearing my name blurted out in Dutch. I quickly gauged that nobody could understand a fucking word I was saying. I'd read a bit about racial tensions in Belgium and banged on about that for a bit, only realising later that it was actually something I'd read about Germany. Basically, I am now recognisable on the streets of Belgium as somebody who's been on telly doing an impression of the Elephant Man having a nervous breakdown.

Eventually, I moved to London but strictly just for the short term. It was a shame to leave Scotland as it was actually an interesting time in Scottish politics. Apparently Tommy Sheridan had a bug put in his car. I'd love it if it turned out it had been put there by his wife. You have to respect any man so keen to look like the rest of the proletariat that he will toast his own body. At certain points in his basting cycle it used to look like the Scottish Parliament was being addressed by a jobbie with a face. Yet he seemed to be one of the few politicians who cared about the people he represented. I remember hearing a radio phone-in show he did for a bit. There were lots of people phoning in complaining about the state of their back courts and so on. He'd discuss everything as being of equal importance, whether what got brought up was the euro or someone's benefit problems. It's a rare politician who can understand that you don't give a toss about the Maastricht Treaty if your giro hasn't turned up. It was a great show, especially for Scotland, where the benchmark in radio entertainment is usually some tit with a mullet phoning up Greggs and pretending that he's Sean Connery.

It was also around this time that the SNP won the Scottish Parliamentary election, but much was being made of the fact that despite the fact that the SNP was in power, there was no real 'buzz' about independence. 'People aren't really talking about it in the streets,' we were told. This kind of skirts round the fact that this is Scotland, so people aren't really talking to each other much in general. We're a country that knows that people need to choose the right moment to open up to one another. Ideally when one of us is drunk and the other one is dying.

Perhaps independence will one day mean that Scots who have gone south to seek their fortune return home – leaving our streets choked with tramps. If we could repeat our successes of the past in the fields of science and industry then anything might be possible. We could harness our amazing natural-energy resources, and then divert those resources into building a Terminator we can send back through time to kill Geoff Hurst's mum.

At least Alex Salmond looks Scottish, as if his heart pumps about once a day and his liver is fighting the Alamo. I suspect that, like Moses, he will not be the one to lead us into the Promised Land, although I do think he makes an interesting leader. If only for the excitement of seeing how long a man can survive under that pressure with the cholesterol levels of a fried egg. He looks like a self-satisfied cat that's about to ask you a riddle. It's surely a measure of his ability that I seem to remember him standing down for a few years but have no memory of who replaced him. The Nationalists may as well have spent a couple of years being led by an animatronic eagle, for all I remember of that man (or perhaps woman).

I quite surprised myself by starting to go to musicals in London. Yes, I know. Some people just hate them. That musical theatre dumbs things down is well illustrated by the fact people now refer to the French literary classic as 'Les Mis'. It's like *Les Misérables* is too much of a downer. Let's start referring to *The Grapes of Wrath* as 'Grapey Wrathy', or *Crime and Punishment* as 'Ruski Murder Funtime'. Personally I just think that musicals are good for the economy. Airlines and hairdressing salons can't physically employ all of Britain's homosexuals.

Of course, some people ask how many more musicals do we have to put up with before Andrew Lloyd Webber can actually afford that plastic surgery? A lot of prejudice against musical theatre comes from people looking at Andrew Lloyd Webber and going, 'My God, you are so ugly.' But just because a man looks like his face was carved off his skull by a diseased butcher, put in a piñata, beaten for six hours with a hockey stick, and the resulting slop piped back onto his head like icing on the ugliest cake the world has ever seen – sorry, I've forgotten my point. But I've always tried to find the positive in everything, and musicals are no different. If it weren't for Elaine Paige then there would never have been a toilet break during *The Two Ronnies*.

I actually prefer musicals to the theatre. You need the songs because that's when you can eat your sweets. Imagine sitting through a Harold Pinter play trying to get through a bag of Maltesers. Waiting through all the pauses just so you could finally have a crunch. You'd never be able to relax.

The following year, *Mock the Week* moved to having a longer run in the summer. When there's fuck-all news. Basically it starts just as parliament closes and ends just as the party-conference season starts. It was particularly awkward for me as I'd already booked myself in to the annual howl of inchoate horror that is the Edinburgh Festival. I did my show most of the week, and would take the train down to London on Mondays and Tuesdays to film *Mock the Week*. The train really started to do my head in. Perhaps after so many years of doing it I'd just run out of patience. It seemed that the GNER has bought some stock from 1950s Russia, which rattled down to London like a dying breath. Actually, the West Coast Line from Glasgow to London has just been finished after ten years. They had to build the tracks just in front of the 9.20 to Euston that left in 1998, and managed to get in ten minutes early.

While commuting on the trains I started to become aware of things you would only notice through extreme boredom. Like the way women hate travelling facing backwards because of primal memories of being carried away from their settlement on the shoulders of Vikings. Then there are the announcements every ten minutes about what's available in the buffet car. We know what'll be available in the buffet car. It'll be the sort of stuff that's always available in a buffet car. We'll be surprised if you don't sell crisps, we'll be surprised if you've got a roast duck on a rotisserie spit.

Miles Jupp is one of the few people who hates trains more than me, having a higher innate sense of what being treated decently entails. A few years earlier we wrote some sketches for a radio pilot and all the sketches reflected our shared horror at trying to interface with the world. Here's one of them that was set in a railway ticket office.

Attendant: Next.
Traveller: Can I have a ticket to Salisbury, please?
Attendant: Ah yes, it's lovely at this time of year. No, hang on, that's last month I was thinking of. And I wasn't thinking of Salisbury, I was thinking of the Dominican Republic. Smoking or non-smoking?
Traveller: Non-smoking, please
Attendant: Oh, they're all smoking.
Traveller: Well, why did you say smoking or non-smoking then?
Attendant: We pride ourselves on always offering a choice.

Traveller: Right, well can I get a ticket please?

Attendant: Single or return?

Traveller: How much more is the return?

Attendant: It's not more – it's less.

Traveller: Really?

Attendant: Yes.

Traveller: Well, I'm not planning on returning, but if it's cheaper ...

Attendant: Oh no. You have to return.

Traveller: Why?

Attendant: Because when you get to Salisbury the doors don't open. It just comes straight back.

Traveller: The doors don't open?

Attendant: Not at stations, no. They're open for the rest of the journey. They have to be. Everybody's smoking. It would become unbearable.

Traveller: Is there any benefit in getting this train at all?

Attendant: There is a trolley service.

Traveller: If I get a single then? Will I be able to get off at Salisbury?

Attendant: Oh yes. Not the station itself obviously, but if you time your jump right you could land pretty near to the station.

Traveller: So none of you trains actually stop at Salisbury station?

Attendant: No. They used to. But we had a lot of problems with people getting on and off.

Traveller: Look, is there any way I can get to Salisbury safely? Is there a bus service?

Attendant: Sir, this is a TRAIN station. Would you go into a baker's and ask for a handful of meat? Would you leave a note on your doorstep saying 'Dear Mr Travel Agent, two first-class flights to Orlando'??

Traveller: Please can I just buy a train ticket to Salisbury!?

Attendant: I'm sorry, we close at half-past two.

Traveller: Well, what have you been doing for the last ten minutes.

Attendant: Humouring you.

Traveller: No you haven't.

Attendant: Sorry, my mistake. I've been humouring myself. Now, if you'll excuse me, I have to write a letter to my MP asking for three pints of semi-skimmed milk and a yoghurt.

Obviously Scottish trains have given me some glimpses of Lovecraftian horror. Like the time I saw a businessman trying to chat a woman up by telling her about a free-kick he'd scored at five-a-side that lunchtime.

'Bang. Right in the top corner, darling.'

Or the drunken bams who met at my table on a train to Aberdeen and explicitly and loudly agreed to shag each other when they got off the train.

'Life's too short,' the woman drawled at me. It will be for you, you AIDS-chasing scumbag.

Having done the festival for a number of years, I always try to stay out of it as much as possible. Like a lot of locals, I find it a bit of a pain in the arse. Yes, it's good that you can go to see some great shows but having your city look like the evacuation of Saigon is a pretty high price to pay for that. One week, I played a couple of late-night shows at the EICC. There were break dancers on before me. The predominantly Scottish crowd were pretty amazed, but then it was definitely the first time they had seen more than one black person in a room.

I have to say that during the festival the late shows generally start to bite. These are the gigs you do to try to plug your show, or make a bit of spending money. I usually have a Red Bull before every show but it always catches up with me. I always looked forward to the final week of the festival when I struggle to speak because my throat contains my own poisoned pancreas.

That year, I took the unusual step of employing a boy on work experience. He wanted to learn how to become a comedian, so I took him to a bunch of shows to train him up. Hopefully he can replace me after the heart attack/stroke/lone gunman that is surely just around the corner now. I would honestly love to franchise my act out and let someone like this kid take the bullet/lawsuit/fatal sexual disease that I so richly deserve. A lot of comics kindly agreed to talk to him about what they do. While secretly suspecting that I am a predatory homosexual. For all the industry bullshitters in town, at some level the Fringe is still like a medieval circus for the performers. Subconsciously, we are allowing promoters, agents, venues to make a lot of money from us in exchange for us being allowed to get wrecked for a month.

I have to say that I find the adverts of a lot of female performers at the festival depressingly sexualised. Are these posters telling me I should go to see someone just because they have nice tits? I will, and that makes it even worse. It would be good to see a female performer who had the courage to have a poster where their looks weren't used as a selling point. That would turn me on even more.

Not learning is clearly quite a big part of my personality. I've always hated doing festivals, so I went to Ireland for the Kilkenny Festival. I made the mistake of flying, despite being utterly terrified. I've never managed to overcome my fear – generally there's nowhere I want to visit so much that I'm willing to be fired towards it in a tin box full of other people's farts.

The security now is as frightening as the flight. You're not allowed to bring fluids on the plane in case you make an improvised bomb from Coca-Cola and iPod parts. Who's training Al-Qaida these days, Johnny Ball? If you really want to bring a plane down, get a normal bottle of Sunny Delight and shake it. Of course, airport security is even tighter if you look vaguely Middle Eastern. If you've got a turban and a beard, you're about six months away from having to fly naked on a clear plastic plane.

I can't begin to explain the different levels of increasingly wild paranoia that flying brings out in me. You think you're scared of flying? Frightened of turbulence maybe? I panic every second of the ascent as I fear that the plane might contain an altitude-triggered bomb – something that may not even exist, for all I know. I always fear our own government agencies more than 'terrorists'. You're looking for possible Muslim extremists on your flight? I'm looking for guys who look like they used to be in the army but now have cancer. I spent the whole of the flight to Ireland eyeballing a little bald man who had a quite futuristic pen that I felt might double up as some kind of detonator. He was reading the Bible, which didn't help. People say they find prayer reassuring, but if the pilot came on the intercom and told you to put your seatbelts back on, would you really be happy to hear him tailing off into a few verses of the 'Our Father'? Still, not quite as frightening as him bursting into something from the Koran.

What would be typical behaviour for people who are going to blow up a plane? Apparently, American Airlines are working on cameras which would monitor our faces on flights to check for telltale signs of nervousness. Good job they've not installed those yet. On the flight to Ireland I gave a performance that saw me gibbering like Dustin Hoffman in *Rainman*. I'd currently be doing a ten-year stretch in one of America's underwater prison cities.

After the terror of the flight, I did the Kilkenny Festival with adrenalin levels most people will only ever achieve during a rape. Everybody there is incredibly nice, and the whole thing has a real party feel. Being a non-drinker made me feel like I was keeping one of the thousands of alcoholic comedians on the circuit away from the time of their life. The drinking was astonishing – even to someone from Glasgow. One night I had to hurdle a guy who was on all fours to get into the hotel.

Typically, you do a bunch of shows there over maybe five days. The first one I did was compered by an act that was an Irish guy pretending to be a German. He auctioned off a bunch of those crap CDs you get free with newspapers, some dishcloths and a whole load of car-boot-sale stuff. It went on for ages and he raised something like a few hundred euros. There was a real tension in the crowd as to where he was going with this. Then, quite suddenly, he gave the money to some woman in the front row and fucked off. What a great way to get introduced. I was almost crying with laughter as I walked up. The woman didn't pay any attention while I was on; she was just sitting there wondering why the fuck he'd given her all those euros.

I got back from Kilkenny to the news that Tony Blair had finally stood down as prime minister. I liked those photos the tabloids used to run showing how Tony Blair had aged over his ten years in power. Essentially, we were being ruled by a slightly effeminate talking skeleton. I think that this withering came through his addiction to power. As a weak-willed person drawn towards power his need to 'keep using the Ring' left him shrivelled and spent like Gollum. 'Tricksy Gordon! Nasssty Chancellor! He wants our Preciousss!'

A poll when Blair left said that 69 per cent of people reckoned Blair's legacy would be the Iraq War. I think that ignores his real record of achievement in dismantling the Labour movement. It's amazing to think that the huge effort he went to creating a massive cash-for-honours scandal will be overshadowed. Blair was said to be saddened that he hasn't managed to serve for as many years as Thatcher. Instead he will have to content himself with having killed more women and children than Genghis Khan. Ironically, for a man who is so obsessed with legacy, his memory will live on longer than most politicians – as a ghost story that Iraqi mothers use to frighten their children.

That said, I do think that Blair stands a good chance of success in his new role of Peace Envoy. There's a real chance that all those different groups in the Middle East will join together to try and kill him. In six months time he could be putting an end to years of suffering as he is sacrificed on an altar in the centre of Baghdad while everyone celebrates like it's the end of a *Star Wars* movie. It's said that he might help bring peace to the Middle East in the same way he helped the peace process in Northern Ireland. Then again, he didn't bomb Belfast with depleted uranium shells and hang Gerry Adams in a shed while someone filmed it on a mobile phone. I think that might have put a bit of a dent in the Good Friday Agreement.

I was supposed to fly out to do the Montreal Festival after Kilkenny but cancelled it. I decided that I was never going to fly again and I never have. I feel a lot more relaxed since I made the decision. A lot of what I thought was stress turned out to be simply the horror of having a flight coming up, so I'm delighted to have stopped. Also, I won't be dying in a fireball at minus 60 degrees any time soon. Of course, everyone I met who went to Montreal that year would bang on about how it was the best year ever and how they all got to hang out with Billy Connolly! As the great man himself might have said in my position, 'Fuck Off!'

SIXTEEN

Mock the Week had become inexplicably popular, so I went on a massive tour around Britain. I think it was 135 dates in just over a year. To be honest I lost count, along with my appetite, sex-drive and desire to go on living. We did it in two legs. The Scottish leg had the Reverend Obadiah for support and we drove about in a camper van along with a chef (an art student we recruited at a party) and a masseuse (an art student we recruited at a party). How much damage would you imagine Jim could do to a crappy camper van in three weeks? Six grand you say? Spot on.

The idea was to have some fun and we brought a friend to film it as an extra for the DVD. I'd forgotten that this was Scotland in the middle of winter and we all teetered on the brink of a group nervous breakdown. It seemed like I was the only non-drug user on the tour, so I'd get up and go for bracing morning walks while almost everyone else slept off the combination of ecstasy, cocaine and ketamine apparently know as 'chaos'. The gigs themselves were pretty good. We did a bunch of places nobody had ever heard of bar European funding bodies, who apparently love to throw up a 200-seat theatre in the middle of a wilderness where Ray Mears would starve to death.

We noticed something that set the tone for the whole tour. The shows sold out quickly. I'm really not complaining; the memory of nobody coming to my Fringe shows is a vivid one and I can't say how much I appreciate anyone parting with their money to see me. Trouble was, everything gets sold on the internet nowadays, so the people who'd get the tickets were worthy, organised types, the opposite of my target audience. I'd try to bam up front rows that were entirely composed of slightly different types of accountant. The shows still went well, but I got the feeling that the people who would have really loved it, the stoners and Goths and nutjobs, just weren't in the room.

The second leg was in England with my good friend Martin Bigpig. Martin is a big, tattooed Irishman with an enormous red beard. He started out in circuses and then went into street-performing. Finally, he went into comedy and it seemed like a piece of piss because he didn't have to juggle anything sharp or burning, or ride a unicycle while he did it. When I was starting out, Martin was the comedian who influenced me the most. He brought the mixture of audience stuff and prepared stuff that worked in street-performance into the world of club comedy. The sort of structure that you see a lot of acts working with now – doing audience stuff, and having bits of their acts where they can refer back to audience characters they've built up – is something that he brought to alternative comedy. Of course there was a little bit of stuff like that going on anyway, but I honestly think comedy clubs would be a fair bit different today without Martin.

We're good mates and I'd say Martin is pretty upbeat, buoyant even, and I'm not, but I am pretty philosophical. Even so, the tour was absolutely fucking harrowing. Martin got me through it in the way that an explorer might haul his friend's corpse out of a jungle. The relentless travelling and Chinese food took its toll, and we started to go to the hotel gyms and pools every day as we sensed the real possibility that the tour might break us.

We tried to think of anybody who toured a lot and still looked fit, deciding that if we just asked ourselves what they would do in any given scenario we would be able to survive the whole thing. Bruce Springsteen was who we settled on and we genuinely made every decision from then on based around what we thought he might do. Often we would waste quite a bit of time when we should have been in the gym arguing about whether Bruce Springsteen would get a sandwich from a garage, or whether he'd try to find a restaurant in the next town.

We had a fictitious tour manager who we'd talk endlessly about as well. Little Chris was a huge, black American guy who had always just left when you came into a room. We'd regale each other with stories about how much he'd hated breakfast, or how he'd popped out to set up our afterparty in Telford. If that tour had lasted five more dates we'd have killed someone.

One problem we had was that people just kept going for a piss during the gigs. Some of those shows were like a bedwetters' convention. In York, there was loads of heckling which was fun at first, and just everybody kept incessantly going to the toilet. I think people were starting to enjoy getting laid into. Trouble is after about the thirtieth time there's really not much more you can say about it and it really disturbed the rhythm of the show. At the end, I went into a big, long bit about how I had a part in a movie where I play a character from York. I told them I had a voice coach and had been working really hard on getting the accent just right, asking would it be OK if I tried it out to see what they thought. Misguidedly, I then went into a really prolonged impression of a spastic. Still getting hate mail from York.

It was only a short while into the tour when my second child was born. My partner really wanted me to be involved in the birth so there was a particularly horrible build-up. One day, we got the bus to an old woman's house and she gave us a mad talk about childbirth. This involved her putting on Native American music (it wasn't called America till Whitey got there. I hate this term and prefer the more politically correct Genocidal Residue. Fuck it, let's go with Red Indian) and then lying on the floor, splaying her legs and holding an actual human pelvis, from a skeleton, over her fanny. That afternoon really went by quite slowly. Also, I'm not sure that the Red Indians had access to reverb technology. I'm sure those CDs are overproduced.

On the day my son was born I came back from a show, sat in the hospital through the labour, then had to go do another show a couple of hours after he was born. I said to everybody that obviously it wasn't as hard as giving birth. Actually, I felt that it was. Doing the show right after the birth was really weird, running through jokes like I was in a dream and just hoping the right words would come out. I was in the same clothes that I'd been in since the previous night. I said to my partner that the audience could probably smell me. She laughed, 'They could probably smell me.'

Earlier this year a 66-year-old woman became the oldest new mum in Britain after giving birth to a baby boy. I'm amazed she needed to have a Caesarean section though – you'd think at 66 she would have needed some masking tape down there just to stop it falling out. She said the most important thing is that she is able to give the baby a normal, happy childhood. Which he will have – right up until she dies. It's going to be unusual having someone in their 70s picking up a child from school who's not a paedophile.

I've been touring a lot since my children were born but I still think I've raised them well. The most important thing for a young child is that they get to use their imagination. If their daddy's not there, that leaves a hell of a lot to the imagination. Also, any time they write and ask me about myself, I say I'm a Transformer. Let their little minds run riot! But at least I'm not like the father of Chantelle Steadman's baby. DNA tests proved that 13-year-old Alfie Patten was not the father and that the actual dad, 15-year-old Tyler Barker, was facing up to the 'reality of fatherhood'. That's if your definition of fatherhood is being a child who neither supports nor lives with his baby who's gone into hiding with her nationally infamous 15-year-old mother. His experience of fatherhood couldn't be less like reality if he birthed a child from his right thigh and left it to be suckled by mountain lions. He said that he and his girlfriend were going to share the looking after of their child – share it with the social services, that is. It could be the first case of a child being taken into care with their parents. As the girl may have slept with other young boys, Eastbourne

Council demanded a paternity test. Why? So the CSA can demand they pay three packets of 'Monster Munch' a week in maintenance? David Cameron said he blamed Gordon Brown! Christ, is there anyone this girl hasn't slept with?

My tour ended on a fairly bizarre note. The final gigs were at the Hammersmith Apollo in December 2008. Right at the start of the show a drunk ran up onstage dressed as Santa. I made it clear I wasn't particularly amused and eventually he turned round and started to dismount from the high stage. Seizing the moment I gave him a cowardly shove in the back, so he landed painfully on the floor. As I turned to the baffled crowd I saw the shocked face of a 10-year-old boy, who'd just watched me scream 'Fuck off!' at Santa.

When the DVD of my tour launched, I entered show business properly for the first time, and was doing the endless, pointless interviews with local radio and phone interviews with the *Daily Star*'s TV supplement. The real problem, other than the fact that nobody reads, listens to or cares about any of this shit, was that after talking to more than two or three people I would invariably lose it and start lying or just spouting the plots of my favourite comic books as if they were things that have happened to me. I sat in an office in a warehouse on an industrial estate going pretty full-on mental for about a week. Here's an example of a phone-interview transcript:

1. Who's your favourite *Star Wars* character, and why?

C-3PO, although I hate it when he rapes those student nurses. Often, when I talk about this to friends, we wonder if it was actually *Star Wars* that I watched.

2. When were you last sick?

Towards the end of a brutal bestiality scene in what may have been *The Empire Strikes Back*.

3. If you could have a super power, what would it be?

To travel between the dimensions at will, always uncertain whether my power is actually just schizophrenia.

4. Would you rather have no legs or no arms?

I reckon no arms would be easier as I could still keep my hobbies, hillwalking and masturbating with my feet.

5. What makes a kick-arse night out kick proper arse?

Ecstasy. I'm supposed to say good mates or something, right? On ecstasy I could have a kick-arse night out with Ronan Keating and Ariel Sharon.

6. What is the first album you ever bought?

Buddy Holly's *Greatest Hits* in Woolworth's. The assistant sniggered at me for buying it, but later that year she was bending over stacking shelves and I saw one of her tits. Swings and roundabouts.

7. What would your funeral be like?

A zombie-themed fancy-dress affair where the mourners eat rice pudding from my open skull.

8. Who's the biggest arsehole famous person you've ever met?

I try to see the good in everyone. I struggled a bit with Dom Joly though, the talentless fat cunt.

9. Have you got any phobias?

I am terrified of heterosexuals, going senile and heterosexuals.

10. Without looking, how many MySpace friends have you got?

Thousands – and I'm certain that one day one of them will kill me. Unless I start wearing a condom.

11. What's the worst idea you've ever had?

Killing Jill Dando.

12. What's the stupidest thing you've ever said to a girl you liked?

'Jill, I think Crete is a marvellous holiday destination. If you don't give it a good review, who knows what I'll do.'

13. What's the most illegal thing you (or 'a friend of yours') have ever done?

Probably a bit of bullying I did on a little ginger kid at school. Not technically illegal until they can produce a body. As I tell his family when they picket my gigs, he might have just run away.

14. What have you seen that you really wish you could un-see?

Bonekickers.

15. What's the worst injury you've ever received, and how did it happen?

I once broke my wrist trying to mime the word 'fisting' during charades.

16. Why should people buy your new DVD?

It's pretty much a shot-for-shot remake of *The Poseidon Adventure*, but with mice.

17. What's the punch line to your favourite-ever joke?

'That's the last time I do any experiments on … GIANT CRAB ISLAND!!!'

It was around this time that the whole Jonathan Ross/Russell Brand debacle was hitting the news, and I got dragged into it by a variety of idiots. Russell Brand is actually one of my favourite celebrities. The manner of his death will give Michael Hutchence back his dignity. I think that whole 'debate' was just a distraction from the banking crisis, the war and the looming recession. It was something everybody could have an opinion about that we all knew didn't actually matter in the real world, where things had just started to look pretty scary. Anyway, the Director-General of the BBC was on *Newsnight* and the presenter brought up me doing a gag on *Mock the Week*. It was 'Things the Queen Wouldn't Say' and I'd said something along the lines of 'I am now so old that my pussy is haunted'. The Director-General gave a look much like someone had set fire to his arse hair. For anyone who wasn't a broken-spirited, thought-collar-wearing shitsack of conformity, the whole thing was quite a good laugh really. Anyway, it was a joke that went out about two years ago. My argument would be that if the Queen's pussy wasn't haunted then, it must be by now.

I find it amusing just how touchy some people are about royal jokes. I mean, what year is this? Who gives a fuck about the royals? They're innately ridiculous and, according to David

Icke, big white superlizards with shovel-shaped heads in their transformed state. People say the royals are inbred and I can see why. Look what happens when they try to widen the gene pool – a couple of deaths, a ginger son and a marriage to a horse. Earlier this year the Queen opted to celebrate her 83rd birthday with a simple meal rather than having a lavish banquet, so that she didn't appear out of touch during the credit crunch. It's hardly a show of solidarity with those affected by the recession when she'd be eating while wearing a crown and sitting on a throne inside a palace. Hope she enjoyed her swan-flavoured crispy pancakes. Next, people will be suggesting that her having two birthdays a year makes her elitist.

The whole Ross/Brand thing just seemed disproportionate anyway. It reminded me of a great article where Jon Ronson described the popularity of David Icke as 'part of a larger back-lash against rational thought'. Manuel was a great character but can you imagine *Fawlty Towers* being made today? Every episode would just be thirty minutes of a Polish waitress in a bedsit crying.

In response to the climate of censorship I have created a computer program called 'The *Daily Mail* Random Headline Generator'. It lets you feed in all the recent front-page headlines from the *Daily Mail* and uses the information to predict the next one. I popped it on this morning. It looks like next Monday's front page will be 'Asylum Seekers Carry a New Type of AIDS which Lowers House Prices'.

That said, I was quite lucky with my last DVD. The only thing that was withdrawn for legal reasons was a section about sham-kidnap munter Shannon Matthews. The thing that's surprised me most about that whole thing is that with her family background Shannon Matthews wasn't a cyclops. I don't believe Karen Matthews knew where Shannon was. I'd be amazed if she knows where any of her kids are.

The launch of the DVD meant that when I sat down to start writing the following year, I had to say goodbye to a lot of jokes. But with President Obama getting elected it seemed a great time to be writing some new topical stuff. Obama had just been given high approval ratings but then again he did follow Bush. You could put a brain tumour in the Oval Office and it'd get better ratings. And construct better sentences. Obama's not infallible though – he apologised after his plane swooped low over Ground Zero for a calendar photo. Which is like Gordon Brown posing on the District Line with peroxide and a fuse.

Shortly after he was elected, Obama invited Gordon Brown to a working lunch in Washington. I think Gordon was a bit surprised when he ended up serving bread rolls and pouring the wine. Brown said his meeting with Obama was 'to help sort out the world economic crisis'. The meeting took less than an hour! What exactly did he do? 60 Hail Marys? Gordon did make a speech to Congress though, and it was truly embarrassing. At one point he said, 'With faith in the future let us together, build tomorrow today.'

Is this such a great speech? It sounds like it's been cobbled together on the plane from the clues of *The Times* crossword. 'Outgoing partners once left home to catch a Rolling Stone.' Applause. 'The Spanish ambassador fools about with Mickey Mouse.' Standing ovation. He received nineteen standing ovations in total. I've always thought a standing ovation is a strange thing. 'I'm enjoying what you said so much I'm going to clap, not louder, but higher than before.' The problem is what do you do after the first few standing ovations if the speaker makes a point that you like even more? Do you jump and clap? Or get on the table? Typically, a standing ovation comes at the end of a speech. Essentially the Congressmen tried to get him to finish nineteen times. I mean, why would anyone want to listen to a man whose own country is in meltdown? It's like Fred Goodwin starting a Christmas Club. While in America, Brown also announced that Edward Kennedy would receive an honorary knighthood from Britain. This is a man who fled a car accident in 1969 that led to the death of Mary Jo Kopechne. He doesn't deserve a knighthood. A liar, a coward and a criminal. Sounds more like a Lord to me.

After my tour ended I decided to move back to Scotland. It's been a real relief. I hated the intensity of life in London – walking around a Scottish city is like walking around London after an apocalyptic viral event. I knew that I really needed to get out when Boris Johnson got elected. Voting for Boris Johnson can't have been that different from voting for a Labrador wearing a Wonder Woman costume. He's sort of like a wee boy who's woken up in his dad's body. The Labour Party must really be in trouble if they can lose control of London to a fat albino with Down's syndrome. Earlier this year Madame Tussauds unveiled a waxwork of Boris Johnson. It's so lifelike the only way to tell them apart is that the waxwork is slightly better at running London. I mean, what a waste of money. Boris does so little work he'd have been happy to go down to Madame Tussauds for a couple of hours a day and just stand.

Boris's election made it clear that it's time we went for an entirely different system of government altogether. How about instead of voting, we all write two- to three-hundred-word essays about how we'd generally like things to go. Then we appoint a random celebrity – Jeremy Clarkson or that guy from *The Kumars* – and they have to work their way through what we've written and make as much of it happen as possible. Often the things we'd write would be contradictory, so much of the government's work would involve things like ripping up all the roads and then building them all again. Then, at the end of their term of office, we would burn our leaders alive, just like the old Celtic tribes did (to be honest my source here is Slaine in the comic *2000 AD*). Yes, it's a voting system that would very probably return our nation to the Dark Ages. On the other hand, we'd get to kill Clarkson! Is everybody in?

Since moving back I've realised there's lots of bizarreness in Glasgow, particularly if you've spent your whole life looking for it. Queen's Park has a disturbing Victorian Insect Museum. That's something I'd avoid if you were on drugs. Or recommend. Really, it depends on the drugs. Probably avoid. The park also has a big flagpole where there's a beautiful view out across the city. Anytime I go there somebody clearly on drugs comes up and raves almost stereotypical mentalness at me. One time it was a guy telling me to make a tinfoil helmet to stop the government reading my mind. I moaned at Jim for several minutes about the way somebody on drugs always comes up and spoils that view before I remembered that I was also on drugs.

I moved back to Scotland the week that Barry Ferguson and Allan McGregor were thrown out of the Scottish football team as they were deemed unfit to represent our country. I dunno – I think a couple of drunks making obscene gestures at a crowd of strangers represent our country pretty accurately. We've had to put up with drunk or abusive Scots representing our country in the fields of cinema, cuisine and international diplomacy ... and football is where they draw the line?

Since I got back to Scotland I do find that I'm a bit more recognisable, but probably only in that vague way that makes people think I'm probably somebody who owes them money. I was out camping a couple of months ago and some old guy followed me through the woods and back to my tent, sticking his head in and asking for an autograph for his son. I wrote, 'I fucked your Dad. As we came, we both thought of you' and folded it up nice and tight.

I moved back to Scotland in time to see my daughter finish nursery. They had a cute little graduation ceremony and she sang a song about the continents. I lurked in the background with my boy, both of us drawn by the strange attractor of the buffet. We looked like two guys who didn't care how many continents there were. Afterwards, one of the nursery assistants came by with a plate of cake. I snatched a big bit with a cry of 'Cake!' and bit into it. 'That cake is for the children,' she grimaced. I tried to make light of it by saying, 'All the sweeter!' but blew crumbs everywhere as I did so. It's so rare we get to see ourselves as others see us. That was a tragic time for it to finally happen for me. Still, I love icing. I read that once a wild bear starts coming into a town they have to go and capture it and release it hundreds of miles away. Basically once the bear has tasted peanut butter there's nothing in nature that's going to top that, so they'll always come back. I feel like that myself. I know there's cake out there, so it's hard to eat salad. Look at the stuff we have access to! Who wouldn't feel like a bear? If your neighbour's bin had a tub of choc-choc-chip ice cream in it would you tear it apart like a bear to get at it? Of course you would! I'd fuck a bear! Rrragggghh! Ice cream!

Sometimes I wish I had more of a regular routine to my life, but a lot of the time I do enjoy the weirdness. I did a weekend recently that involved doing a show at some freakish ball in London, then driving to Switzerland and doing a gig in Geneva. At the ball I wandered round the wonderful grounds of the country club it was being held in and enjoyed the snotty looks from real members. How do you get to the stage where you can look down your nose at somebody wearing a tuxedo?

There was a huge glass atrium in the room in which I was playing. In a fit of boredom, I pretended that my contract specifically excluded me from playing atriums. 'No atriums! Did you guys get the old contract or something?' Just before I was due to go on I stuck my head out the back door for some air and swallowed the most enormous moth. I could hear the guy who was going to introduce me talking me up while I knelt on the steps trying to vomit up a living creature that was thrumming somewhere in my vocal cords. It was horrendous. I puked something that looked like a cross between a bat and a tumour, then did the gig sounding like I'd just survived a house-fire.

My friend Craig Campbell met me at the club and drove me to Geneva. To pass the time he played lectures on the philosophy of the mind. An American gentleman, speaking patiently for several hours, finally made me appreciate that my body might not exist. We grabbed a couple of hours sleep in a lay-by. As I got out and stretched beside all the big trucks, I saw for the first time how liberating the life of an itinerant serial killer might be. You could work your way through all kinds of lectures, have an exercise programme you could do in a motorway toilet and just really develop your own style. I might not even kill some days, I reasoned as I breakfasted on a Cornetto.

Geneva is a strange place. The streets were full of ridiculously beautiful women. Perhaps beautiful women are very good at working in the finance industry; that's one option. Or a lot of ugly guys use the money they make in the finance industry to lure beautiful women there. I honestly can't decide. The gig was one of those typical expat things where everybody was sat with their boss. I think expats are chosen for their ability to tolerate bosses. Could you imagine British bosses going out with their staff every weekend? The only boss who should do that is somebody leading a team of behavioural scientists exploring the exact moment when banter turns to violence.

Sometimes I think doing open spots doesn't really tell me that much. Either it's a nice crowd and they laugh at everything, or it's not and they don't. I had to do every open spot in Scotland to get myself match-fit for this year's series of *Mock the Week*. I did a 'Best of Irish' comedy night and pretended to be Irish. 'Like all Irish people, I'm mad for the racism!' That was my catch-phrase, which they hated. A guy came up to me after that and introduced himself as the best impressionist in Scotland.

'Do you watch *Family Guy*?' he asked, in what may have been the voice of a *Family Guy* character.

'No, I don't, I've never seen it.'

'You don't watch *Family Guy*?' he shouted, in what was clearly supposed to be the voice of another *Family Guy* character. 'Geez, I can't believe you don't watch *Family Guy*!' He said that in an English voice that I think may be the voice of the *Family Guy* dog, or perhaps baby.

'I don't have a TV, mate.'

'You know who else doesn't watch TV ...? Robert De Niro. Hey, what you lookin at ...?'

I hid in the toilet while I heard him ask for me in the voice of Robert De Niro and then somebody else I couldn't identify.

At my shows, I always like to have as many Scottish people as possible. Not for nationalistic reasons, but because a largely English audience means that I won't be able to spend about a third of the show throwing lazy, clumsy blows at the city of Dundee. Hats off to Dundonians, they can certainly laugh at themselves. Although, looking around their city, maybe they just love any kind of punishment. It's the sort of place you imagine everyone would have put all their lights on during the Blitz. It's their fire brigade I feel sorry for. Very difficult to do your job properly when the locals are queuing up to throw themselves into the flames.

Another thing I've been doing since I moved back is writing a pilot for a sketch show with Jim and our friend Tom Stade. Tom is a laid-back cannabis-defined Canadian whose natural joyousness and extrovert nature terrifies the people of Scotland. I've stood patiently in a café as he's attempted to get an elderly waitress to high-five him. His joshing good nature is often ignored by Scottish people in the hope that he will fuck off. He never notices because of his joshing good nature. We've all written stuff together that's easily as mental as anything Jim and I used to come up with back at peak ecstasy consumption. That's made me very happy. I suppose I always feared that if I went off and did straight stand-up and panel shows that maybe when I came back the magic wouldn't be there. The magic is still there! The fact that we are the only people who think it's magic is irrelevant.

The other day Jim reminded me of a Dr Presley sketch that went out where Dr Presley controls a defeated-looking grown-up version of the kid from *The Wonder Years*.

'Enough, Fred Savage! I hold your heart within a Perspex cube!'

As I remember, it was delivered as a booming psychic voiceover. Clearly the world needs more of that kind of thing.

I'm also writing my new touring show, which is called 'I Would Happily Punch Every One of You in the Face'. Writing it involves a lot of going to comedy clubs and finding out that a lot of things I thought were funny are actually not funny and don't even make any sense. I can't tell you how much I look forward to the end of this brutal 'pre-season' bit. It will be a relief to get down to talking some serious rubbish on a nightly basis while energy drinks destroy my health and sanity. Oh no, wait a minute, it'll be worse. Still, the good news is I can't live for ever.

At least it's now a really good time to be a topical comedian with a dystopian worldview. Never has everything seemed to be going to fuck with quite such alacrity. The Bank of England has started printing £75 billion of new money to pump into Britain's economy. Soon the banks will start lending again and people will have more cash in their pockets – it's just unfortunate that a Mars bar will cost over £1 million. I don't think we've got anything to worry about though. Printing money may not have worked in Zimbabwe or Nazi Germany, but third time lucky eh? The one bright spot in the financial crisis was when the Chancellor announced in his budget that 'I'm taking the necessary measures for Britain's recovery'. Unfortunately the gun jammed when he tried to shoot himself in the head.

With everyone watching what they spend, Lidl is becoming the most successful supermarket in the UK. The Germans have finally won. They swore in 1940 they would have us all eating bratwurst and finally they've managed it. It's all the strange German food that amuses me. Lidl is full of the kind of people who go on holiday but eat chips because they are scared of foreign food ... and there they are, being forced by their poverty to buy herring in some freaky, day-glo yellow sauce, and sausages that look so like your childhood imaginings of an alien's cock.

Not that you catch a politician in Lidl, of course. It was the *Daily Telegraph* that printed MPs' expense claims and its readers were furious. They have to pay for their own chandeliers, tennis courts and moat cleaning. What I'd like to know is if MPs can claim for all those things, then what aren't they allowed to claim for? Chocolate fountains? Cream horns? Golden baths? Or are all these sexual practices allowed too? Douglas Hogg claimed to have his moat cleaned and Michael Spicer claimed to trim the hedge around his helipad. They couldn't have made the Conservative Party look any more like aristocratic idiots if they'd claimed cash for 'a termination for the scullery-maid and a third-class ticket for her crossing to New Amsterdam'.

Trying to defuse the crisis, Gordon Brown appeared on YouTube – and that's what everyone said when they saw it. Apparently Gordon Brown wore make-up to cover up his blemishes and wrinkles. Christ, what does he look like without make-up on? ET with skin cancer? If an alien skinned a fat man to wear his flesh as a suit would it really look any different from Brown? He's now so wrinkled he looks like Sid James's nutsack. Brown looked like a man getting a prostrate exam from Freddy Krueger. The last time I saw someone looking that fake and uncomfortable on YouTube they were telling us that they were being treated well by their captors. I mean, someone really should tell Brown to stop smiling – it just looks like he's trying to shit a sea urchin. Where did Brown learn to smile? Watching *The Shining*? John Prescott said Brown had 'the worst smile in the world'. Obviously there weren't any mirrors about when he was shagging that secretary.

In preparation for the tour I've been trying to get fit as my body had begun to resemble a sort of fleshy landslide. In a moment of madness, I booked some colonic hydrotherapy. I have to start off by saying that it did make me feel better, but I honestly don't know that it was worth the several circles of hell it took me through. For a start, you have to wear paper pants. Never good and in this case ladies' pink paper pants, due to supply-line difficulties. I had naïvely imagined that I would be left to do the actual, well, insertion, myself. No, it's rammed up there by a stranger. As she did it she blurted, 'I'm sorry about this Frankie!' So was I. Essentially, a colonic is a bum abortion and it's very difficult to keep the conversation going with the practitioner. We chatted idly about our hopes for the future, but the fact that she was manoeuvring a hose around in my arse just killed any real chance of rapport.

After the next tour, that's very probably it for me. Getting out of live work and getting out of show business are my priorities. Hopefully when I retire I can find some hobbies that interest me, like prescription med addiction, dread and loneliness. I'd like to be able to write something really good, a film or a novel, but secretly know this would just see me meeting the same cunts on a slightly different basis. You meet some decent-enough people in comedy or telly, but you must never imagine that they are your friends. One must strive for a mindfulness that they could watch you die, right in front of them and feel only a numbed indifference. Or, at best, mildly horny.

When you meet people you admired on TV ten years ago they always seem slightly lobotomised, as if the quality of cocaine they briefly achieved melted their synapses. I think people get addicted to the money, and to having things done for them. As a result, they agree to more and more shit. Can you honestly watch the telly on a Saturday night and say that mankind deserves to survive as a species?

Of course, I am as big a Cunt as anybody. Probably bigger. Well, listen to me show business, and listen good. I may be a Cunt, but this is one Cunt that you're not going to fuck!

A CHAMBERS MANAGEMENT & 4DVD PRESENTATION

FRANKIE BOYLE

I WOULD HAPPILY PUNCH EVERY ONE OF YOU IN THE FACE

BRAND NEW
LIVE SHOW
ON TOUR
IN 2010

FOR UP TO DATE TOUR LISTINGS AND BOOKING INFO VISIT:
WWW.FRANKIEBOYLE.COM & WWW.TICKETMASTER.CO.UK

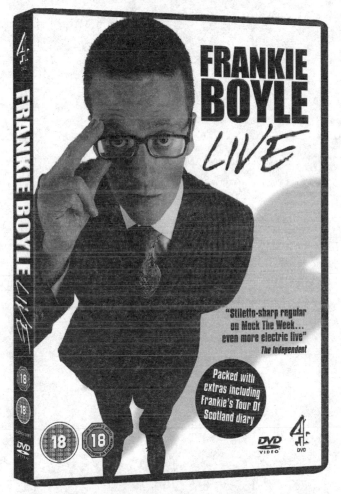